THE COMMON LAW LIBRARY

CHITTY
ON
CONTRACTS

First Supplement
to the
Twenty-Ninth Edition

Up-to-date to July 31, 2004

LONDON
SWEET & MAXWELL
2004

Published in 2004 by
Sweet & Maxwell Limited of
100 Avenue Road London NW3 2PF
http://www.sweetandmaxwell.co.uk
Typeset by Interactive Sciences Limited, Gloucester
Printed in Great Britain by Creative Print and Design (Wales) Ebbw Vale

A CIP catalogue record for this book is available from the British Library

| ISBN Main Work (full set) | 0 421 842601 |
| ISBN Supplement | 0 421 889802 |

[iii]

HOW TO USE THIS SUPPLEMENT

This is the First Supplement to the Twenty-Ninth Edition of *Chitty on Contracts*, and has been compiled according to the structure of the two main work volumes.

At the beginning of each chapter of this supplement the mini table of contents from the main volume has been included. Where a heading in this table of contents has been marked with the symbol ■, the material under that heading has been added to or amended in this first supplement, and should be referred to.

Within each chapter, updating information is referenced to the relevant paragraph in the main volume.

It should be noted, however, that for this Supplement there is no material for chapters 8, 17, 20 and 40.

TABLE OF CONTENTS

VOLUME I

VOLUME II

TABLE OF STATUTES

Where a reference indicates significant discussion of the statute in the text, it is in **bold**. Where a reference is to a footnote, it is *italic*.

TABLE OF STATUTES

TABLE OF STATUTORY INSTRUMENTS

Where a reference indicates significant discussion of the statutory instrument in the text, it is in **bold**. Where a reference is to a footnote, it is *italic*.

TABLE OF NON-UK STATUTORY MATERIAL

Where a reference indicates significant discussion of the legislation in the text, it is in **bold**.
Where a reference is to a footnote, it is *italic*.

TABLE OF CASES

Where a reference indicates significant discussion of the case in the text, it is in **bold**. Where a reference is to a footnote, it is *italic*.

TABLE OF CASES

TABLE OF CASES

TABLE OF EUROPEAN CASES

Where a reference indicates significant discussion of the case in the text, it is in **bold**. Where a reference is to a footnote, it is *italic*.

VOLUME I

GENERAL PRINCIPLES

Part One

INTRODUCTION

Chapter 1

INTRODUCTORY

2. CENTRAL PRINCIPLES OF CONTRACT LAW

(c) *A principle of good faith or contractual fairness?*

Fairness relevant: (2) Implied terms

1–026   *[Add to note 178: page* [23]]
Eastwood v Magnox Electric plc [2004] UKHL 35; [2004] 3 W.L.R. 322 at
[4]–[6].

3. THE HUMAN RIGHTS ACT 1998 AND CONTRACTS

(a) *Contracts made before October 2, 2000*

(i) *The construction and review of legislation governing contracts*

**The impact of sections 3 and 4 of the 1998 Act on accrued contractual
rights**

1–032   *[Add to text at end of paragraph: page* [27]]
On the other hand, in *PW & Co v Milton Gate Investments Ltd*[215a] Neuberger
J. was prepared to accept that s.3 of the Human Rights Act could apply to an
issue arising from a lease made before its coming into force. There, the learned
judge had held that, apart from the operation of s.3, the exercise of a "break
clause" in a head tenancy did not determine the sub-tenancies entered into by the
tenant as permitted under the head-lease even though the head-landlord was
unable to recover rent under the sub-tenancy covenants.[215b] Having referred to a
number of passages in the speeches of their lordships in *Wilson v First County
Trust (No.2)*,[215c] Neuberger J. concluded that their reasoning did not preclude the
application of ss.3 or 4 of the 1998 Act to issues arising out of contracts made
before its coming into force as long as this did not impair "vested rights" or
otherwise create unfairness.[215d] In particular, he noted as "very much in point"
Lord Scott of Foscote's reference in *Wilson's* case to the example of the impact
of legislation intervening between the creation of a lease and its expiry where the
legislation could affect the rights and obligations arising under the transaction.[215e] On the facts before him, Neuberger J. considered that 'the earliest that
any "vested rights" could be said to have arisen under [the break clause in the
head-lease], was the date of the service of the Notice under that clause. Unless
and until [the break clause] was operated, the rights and obligations of any of the
parties as a result of the exercise were merely contingent and not vested.'[215f]
Since this notice had been served after the coming into force of section 3 of the
1998 Act there were no vested rights at the relevant time so as to prevent its
operation on the legislative provisions whose application allegedly prejudiced the
head-landlord's right to property under article 1 of the First Protocol of the
European Convention. Moreover, in the learned judge's view, it was not more
generally unfair to apply section 3 in this way even though the notice had been
served only four days after its coming into force given, in particular, that the 1998

Act had been on the Statute Book for around two years before it came into force.[215g]

[215a] [2003] EWHC 1994 (Ch); [2003] All E.R. (D) 58 (Aug).
[215b] *Ibid.*, at [103]–[104].
[215c] [2003] UKHL 40; [2003] 3 W.L.R. 568.
[215d] *Ibid.*, at [107]–[115].
[215e] [2003] UKHL 40 at [161]; [2003] EWHC 1994 (Ch) at [110] and [114].
[215f] [2003] EWHC 1994 (Ch) at [114].
[215g] *Ibid.*, at [115].

(b) *Contracts made on or after October 2, 2000*

(i) *The construction and review of legislation governing contracts*

Other examples

[Add to text at end of paragraph: page [32]]   **1–041**
    Moreover, in *PW & Co v Milton Gate Investments Ltd*[255a] Neuberger J. accepted the argument of a head-landlord that the effect of ss.139 or 141 of the Law of Property Act 1925 should and could be interpreted so as to prevent the head-landlord from being deprived of rent under the covenants of sub-tenancies which had not determined by the exercise of a "break clause" by the head-tenant. In these circumstances, Art.1 of the First Protocol to the European Convention was engaged: if the underleases would survive the determination of the headlease without the tenant's covenants being enforceable, the head-landlord would be kept out of the premises in question for the remainder of the sub-leases without being able to recover any rent whatever. "That is scarcely 'peaceful enjoyment of [its] possessions.' "[255b]
    In *Ghaidan v Godin Mendoza*[255c] a majority of the House of Lords relied on s.3 of the Human Rights Act 1998 to "read and give effect" to the provisions of the Rent Act 1977[255d] which grants a statutory tenancy to "[t]he surviving spouse (if any) of the original tenant if residing in the dwelling-house immediately before the death of the original tenant" so as to include homosexual cohabitees so as to give effect to their Convention right not to be discriminated against on the ground of sexual orientation in respect of their right to respect for a person's home.[255e] In doing so, their Lordships made a number of important observations on the ambit of the obligation imposed by s.3 of the 1998 Act.[255f]

[255a] [2003] EWHC 1994 (Ch); [2003] All E.R. (D) 58 (Aug).
[255b] *Ibid.*, at [126] *per* Neuberger J.
[255c] [2004] UKHL 30; [2004] 3 W.L.R. 113.
[255d] Rent Act 1977, Sch.I, paras 2 and 3 (as amended).
[255e] European Convention on Human Rights Arts.8 and 14.
[255f] [2004] UKHL 30 esp. [25]–[35] *per* Lord Nicholls of Birkenhead; [38]–[51] *per* Lord Steyn; [104]–[124] *per* Lord Rodger of Earlsferry; *cf.* [57]–[72] *per* Lord Millett (dissenting).

Its impact on duties of confidentiality

[note 307: page [40]]   **1–056**
    Lady Archer v Williams [2003] EWHC 1670 is reported at [2003] E.M.L.R. 38.

5. Contracts Contained In Deeds

(a) *Form and Delivery*

Delivery

1–082   *[Delete text of note 430 from "Once a document" to the end: page* [52] *and insert new text]*

In *Bolton Metropolitan B.C. v Torkington* [2003] EWCA Civ 1634; [2004] Ch. 66 the Court of Appeal held that while s.74(1) of the Law of Property Act 1925 deemed a deed "duly executed" where a corporation's seal is affixed in the presence of and attested by its designated officers, it created no presumption as to its delivery: *ibid.* at [22], [45]. Moreover, while it was not necessary on the facts to decide the point, in Peter Gibson L.J.'s view, at common law "to describe the sealing by a corporation as giving rise to a rebuttable presumption may go too far, implying, as that does, that the burden is on the corporation affixing the seal": *ibid.* at [46]. Where, as on the facts before the court, negotiations were undertaken towards a lease expressly subject to contract, a court should not infer an intention to be bound from the mere sealing of a deed of execution of a lease: *ibid.*, at [53].

6. The Relationship Between Contract And Tort

(c) *Concurrence of Actions in Contract and Tort*

(ii) *Torts Committed in the Course of Performance of a Contract*

Assumption of responsibility

1–120   *[Add new note 659a at end of paragraph: page* [75]]

[659a] *cf. Lennon v Metropolitan Police Commissioner* [2004] EWCA Civ 130; [2004] 2 All E.R. 266 where the principle in *Henderson v Merrett Syndicates* was applied so as to impose liability on a police authority vicariously in respect of its agent's express assumption of responsibility towards one of its constables (technically not being a contractual employee) in respect of the task of transferring him without loss of allowance to another police force.

(d) *The Influence of Contract on Tort beyond Privity*

Subsequent cases

1–162   *[Add at end of note 925: page* [108]]

European International Reinsurance Co Ltd v Curzon Insurance Ltd [2003] EWCA Civ 1074; [2003] Lloyd's Rep. I.R. 793. *cf. Commissioners of Customs & Excise v Barclays Bank plc* [2004] EWHC 122; [2004] 1 Lloyd's Rep. 572 where Colman J. held that the principle of assumption of responsibility was not always a helpful approach to deciding whether a duty of care arose in respect of pure economic loss. He further held that where a freezing injunction has been obtained, the defendant against whom the order has been made does not thereby occupy a relationship of proximity vis-à-vis the claimant, unless there is super-added to the relationship conduct amounting to an assumption of responsibility by that party. Given this, it would be inconsistent to hold that a bank holding the defendant's assets upon being given notice of a freezing injunction thereby owed the claimant a duty of care: *ibid.*, at [73].

Part Two

FORMATION OF CONTRACT

CHAPTER 2

THE AGREEMENT

2. THE OFFER

Offer and invitation to treat

2–006   *[Add new text at end: page* [126]*]*
It has been held that a draft document sent in the course of contractual negotiations with the clear intention of inviting further comment from the recipient was not an offer.[35a]

[35a] *McNicholas Construction Holdings v Endemol UK plc* [2003] EWHC 2472; [2003] E.G.C.S. 136.

3. THE ACCEPTANCE

(a) *Definition*

Negotiation after apparent agreement

[*Add to note 109: page* [135]]   **2–027**
For an application of the principle of looking at the whole correspondence in order to determine whether a contract has been rescinded, see *Drake Insurance plc v Provident Insurance plc* [2003] EWCA Civ 1834; [2004] 2 All E.R. (Comm.) 65 at [100].

6. INCOMPLETE AGREEMENT

Stipulation for the execution of a formal document

[*Add to note 428: page* [175]]   **2–114**
Thoresen & Co (Bangkok) Ltd v Fathom Marine Co [2004] EWHC 167 (Comm.); [2004] 1 All E.R. (Comm.) 935 (agreement for the sale of a ship "sub details" held not to be a binding contract).

[*Add to note 429, line 9 after reference to The Kurnia Dewi: page* [176]]
Harvey Shopfitters Ltd v ADI Ltd [2003] EWCA Civ 1752; [2004] 2 All E.R. 982.

General requirement of "exchange of contracts"

[*Add to note 444: page* [177]]   **2–117**
Secretary of State for Transport v Christos [2003] EWCA Civ 1073 is reported in [2004] 1 P.&C.R. 17.

8. CONDITIONAL AGREEMENTS

(b) *Degrees of Obligation*

Duty not to prevent occurrence of the event

[*Add to note 584: page* [195]]   **2–148**
cf. CEL Group Ltd v Nedlloyd Lines UK Ltd [2003] EWCA Civ 1716; [2004] 1 All E.R. (Comm.) 689 at [11] (where the contract was not in terms conditional but the court applied a similar principle to that stated in Main Work, para.2–148 by virtue of the rule stated in Main Work para.13–012.)

9. CONTRACTUAL INTENTION

Collective agreements

2–171   [*Add to note 699: page* [208]]

For the degree of precision required in the terms of collective agreements to enable their terms to be incorporated in individual employment contracts, see *Kaur v MG Rover Group* [2004] I.R.L.R. 279.

Nature of relationship between the parties

2–175   [*Add to note 719: page* [210]]

cf. Essex Strategic Health Authority v David-John [2003] Lloyd's Rep. Med. 586 (relationship between general practitioner and Health Authority not contractual).

Other cases

2–178   [*Add to note 735: page* [212]]

cf. Sutton v Mishcon Reya [2003] EWHC 3166 (Ch): cohabitation agreement by which one man was to be "slave" to another arguably "just an act or a role-play" (at [26]).

CHAPTER 3

CONSIDERATION

3. Adequacy Of Consideration

Nominal consideration

[*Add to note 94: page* [228]]   **3–019**
    See also Charities Act 1993, s.65(1)(a), requiring "full consideration in money
or money's worth", a requirement not satisfied in *Bayoumi v Women's Total*

Abstinence Educational Union Ltd [2003] EWCA Civ 1548; [2004] 3 All E.R.
110 at [46]–[47].

9. Discharge And Variation Of Contractual Duties

(a) *Variation*

(iii) *Equitable mitigations*

The promise or representation must be "clear" or "unequivocal"

3–090   *[Add to note 386, line 12: page [266]]*
Super Chem Products Ltd v American Life & General Insurance Co Ltd [2004]
UKPC 2; [2004] 2 All E.R. 358 at [23], where the present requirement was not
satisfied.

11. Proprietary Estoppel

(b) *Bases of Liability*

Alternative explanation: contract

3–141   *[Add to note 709: page [303]]*
See also *Oxley v Hiscock* [2004] EWCA Civ 546; [2004] 3 All E.R. 703 at
[35]–[36], distinguishing between cases of proprietary estoppel and those in
which parties *before* acquiring property reach "an agreement, arrangement or
understanding . . . that each is to have a beneficial share in the property."

(c) *Conditions giving rise to liability*

Kinds of promises giving rise to proprietary estoppel

3–143   *[Add to note 719–720: page [305]]*
Secretary of State for Transport v Christos [2003] EWCA Civ 1073 is reported
in [2004] 1 P. & C.R. 17.

12. Special Cases

Novation of partnership debts

3–173   *[Add new text at end: page [324]]*
In *Re Burton Marsden Douglas*[892a] A practised as a solicitor and was
instructed by X to act in the administration of an estate of which X was executor.

After liabilities were incurred by A to X, A went into partnership with B and C. After A had disappeared, it was held that B and C were not responsible for liabilities incurred by A before they had joined the partnership. There had been no novation of A's liabilities incurred before that time since (a) there had been no agreement to novate those liabilities; and (b) there would be no consideration for any promise by B and C to discharge those liabilities since there was no promise by X to release A.

[892a] [2004] EWHC 593 (Ch); [2004] 3 All E.R. 222.

Non-feasance and misfeasance

[Add new text at end: page [326]]   **3–177**
There appears to be an exception to the position stated at the end of this paragraph of the Main Work. The exception is said to arise where A's representation to B that A will take certain steps to safeguard some specific financial interest of B's amounts to an "express assumption of responsibility for a particular matter".[908a] A's failure to exercise due care in discharging that responsibility may then make him liable to B in tort and such liability has been said to cover "acts of omission".[908b]

[908a] *Lennon v Metropolitan Police Commissioner* [2004] EWCA Civ 130; [2004] 2 All E.R. 266 at [34].
[908b] *ibid.*, at [20]. *Quaere*, however, whether the wrongful conduct in *Lennon's* case did not amount to misfeasance in the sense in which that expression is used in para.3–177 of the Main Work (*i.e.*, "failure to achieve a *promised result*").

CHAPTER 4

FORM

2. Contracts For The Sale Or Other Disposition Of An Interest In Land

(b) *The New Law: Contracts made on or after September 27, 1989*

(i) *Contracts within Section 2 of the Law of Property (Miscellaneous Provisions) Act 1989*

Variations

4–056   *[Add new note 262a at end of paragraph: page* [354]]
[262a] *cf. HL Estates Ltd v Parker-Lake Homes Ltd* [2003] EWHD 604 (Ch).

[Add new paragraph: page [354]]
Boundary agreements between neighbours

4–056A   In *Joyce v Rigolli*[262b] the Court of Appeal considered whether a boundary agreement between neighbouring landowners constituted "a contract for the sale or other disposition of an interest in land" within the meaning of s.2 of the Law of Property (Miscellaneous Provisions) Act 1989. In this respect, the court adopted the distinction drawn by Megarry J. in *Neilson v Poole*,[262c] in the context of the requirement of registration of such an agreement as an "estate contract" within s.10(1) of the Land Charges Act 1925, between agreements which constitute an exchange of land and those by which the parties merely intend to "demarcate" an unclear boundary referred to in title documents, "a contract merely to demarcate and confirm [not being] a contract to convey".[262d] According to the Court of Appeal, for a contract to be one "for" selling or disposing of land within the meaning of s.2 of the 1989 Act, "it must have been part of the parties' purposes, or the purposes to be attributed to them, in entering into such a contract that the contract should achieve a sale or other disposition of land. The fact that the effect of their contract is that land or an interest in land is actually conveyed, when that effect was neither foreseen nor intended nor was it something which ought to have been foreseen or intended, is not the acid test."[262e] However, on the facts before them it had been found that while the agreement to establish the boundary did not purport to be a contract to convey any land, one of its parties consciously thought that he was giving up a small amount of land.[262f] Nevertheless, the Court of Appeal held s.2 inapplicable: the important public policy in upholding informal boundary agreements which are "act[s] of peace, quieting strife and averting litigation"[262g] led the court to hold that Parliament could not have intended s.2 to apply to transfers of land pursuant to demarcating boundary agreements simply because a trivial transfer or transfers of land were consciously involved, and it should be presumed, until the contrary is shown, that any transfer of land effected by such an agreement is trivial for this purpose.[262h]

[262b] [2004] EWCA Civ 79; [2004] All E.R. (D) 203 (Feb).
[262c] (1969) 20 P. & C.R. 909.
[262d] *Ibid.*, at [918]–[920].
[262e] [2004] EWCA Civ 79 at [31] *per* Arden L.J.
[262f] *Ibid.*, at [30], [32].
[262g] *Nielson v Poole* (1969) 20 P. & C.R. 909, 919 *per* Megarry J.
[262h] [2004] EWCA Civ 79 at [32]–[34]. cf. *ibid.*, at [45] Sir Martin Nourse referring to "the de minimis principle".

Conditions in planning agreements

[*Page* [356]]   **4–060**
Criticism by *Emmet and Farrand on Title* (19th ed.) para.2–047 of the decision in *Jelson Ltd v Derby City Council*, which required the signature of the housing association, on the basis that s.2 of the 1989 Act requires only the signature of the contracting parties was said to seem valid by Waller L.J. in *Nweze v Nwoko* [2004] EWCA Civ 379; [2004] 2 P. & C.R. D1, *The Times,* May 6, 2004.

Compromises

[*Add to text at end of paragraph: page* [358]]   **4–063**
Similarly, in *Nweze v Nwoko*[295a] the Court of Appeal held that a compromise agreement between two parties to an executed contract of sale of land under which, *inter alia,* the buyer agreed to sell the property with vacant possession at

the best price available on the open market (so as to be in a position to pay the price of the earlier purchase to the sellers) was not a contract *for* the sale or other disposition of an interest in land within the meaning of s.2 of the Law of Property (Miscellaneous Provisions) Act 1989. In doing so, Waller L.J. relied on the Law Commission's Report, *Formalities for Contracts for Sale, etc. of Land*,[295b] which "is clearly concerned with contracts or dispositions under which land or an interest in land is actually sold or disposed of".[295c] While the compromise agreement required the buyer to sell the property (to a third party), it did not itself effect a sale of the property.[295d]

[295a] [2004] EWCA Civ 379; [2004] 2 P. & C.R. D1; *The Times*, May 6, 2004.
[295b] (1987) No. 164.
[295c] [2004] EWCA Civ 379 at [25].
[295d] *Ibid.*, at [31].

Signature

4–069   *[Add at the beginning of note 320: page* [361]]
RG Kensington Management Co v Hutchinson [2002] EWHC 1180; [2003] 2 P. & C.R. 13 (signature by each party to the contract, not each party to the prospective conveyance or transfer).

CHAPTER 5

MISTAKE

2. COMMON MISTAKE

(c) *Mistake at Common Law*

(ii) *Situations in which contract may be void for Common Mistake*

Mistakes as to law

[*Note 163, page* [393]]   **5–042**
The decision of Morland J. in *Brennan v Bolt Burdon* (which in the Main Work
is stated incorrectly: Morland J. held that the compromise agreement was invali-
dated by the mistake of law) was reversed on appeal, [2004] EWCA Civ 1017.
The Court of Appeal accepted that a mistake of law may render a contract void;
the principle underlying the decision in *Kleinwort Benson Ltd v Glasgow City
Council (No. 2)* [1999] 1 A.C. 153 is not confined to restitution (at [12] and [26]).
However, there is not a mistake of law if the relevant law was merely in doubt.

The majority held that in this case the law was merely in doubt; the parties could have discovered that the relevant decision was under appeal.

In addition, when combined with the "declaratory theory of law" espoused in the *Kleinwort* case that when a decision is overturned the previous view of the law was mistaken, the mistake of law rule would threaten the finality of compromise agreements. In the view of Maurice Kay L.J. and Bodey J., a compromise agreement is one under which each party should be treated as accepting the risk that their view of the law might subsequently turn out to be mistaken (at [31] and [39]; *cf.* Main Work, para.5–015). Bodey J. would imply a term to that effect (at [42]). If the parties want to be able to withdraw from the compromise agreement should their view of the law turn out to have been mistaken, they should provide for that expressly (at [22] and [42]).

Sedley L.J. agreed that the appeal should be allowed: "a shift in the law cannot be allowed to undo a compromise of litigation entered into in the knowledge of both of how the law now stood and of the fact—for it is always a fact—that it might not remain so" (at [64]), though he preferred not to base this on an implied term but on the factual matrix of the agreement.

The court left open the question whether a mistake of law could ever invalidate a compromise agreement if, as a matter of construction, the compromise applies (*cf. Bank of Credit and Commerce International SA (In Liquidation) v Ali (No.1)* [2001] UKHL 8; [2002] 1 A.C. 251, in which the House of Lords held that a general release was not effective to release a claim for "stigma" damages that neither party could have known about: see Main Work para.5–012.) To exempt compromises altogether from the mistake of law rule might not be inconsistent with the *Kleinwort* case, as Lord Goff (at p.382G) and Lord Hope (at p.412F–G) had suggested that in a restitution case there might be a defence of "settlement of an honest claim" (at [14], [23] and [30]).

Maurice Kay L.J. doubted if a mistake of law would ever render performance impossible (at [22]). Sedley L.J. considered that in mistake of law cases the test of impossibility was too narrow; he would apply a test of whether the mistake destroyed the subject matter (at [60]).

In *S v S* [2003] Fam 1 it was held that a mistake of law was not a sufficient ground to set aside a consent order made in ancillary relief proceedings, though there was no such mistake on the facts. One ground for the decision, that the *Kleinwort* principle was confined to restitution cases, was rejected in *Brennan v Bolt Burdon* but Maurice Kay L.J. (at [12]) expressed sympathy with the other ground, that public policy favouring an end to litigation must prevail. On consent orders see Main Work, para.5–048, n.200.

3. Mistakes in "Communication"

(c) Unilateral Mistake as to Terms

(ii) Mistaken Identity

5–078—
5–082A   *Shogun Finance Ltd v Hudson* is now reported at [2004] 1 A.C. 919.

CHAPTER 6

MISREPRESENTATION

2. WHAT CONSTITUTES EFFECTIVE MISREPRESENTATION

(b) *Statement by or known to Other Party*

Statements of law

[Note 45a, page [435]]   **6–011**
See this Supplement, para.5–042, above.

The representor

[Add to note 88, page [440]]   **6–020**
An agent may have authority to make representations in relation to a particular transaction even though he has no authority to conclude the transaction: *First Energy v HIB* [1993] 2 Lloyd's Rep. 194, 204; *MCI Worldcom International Inc v Primus Telecommunications plc* [2004] EWCA Civ 957; [2004] All E.R. (D) 418 (Jul) at [25]. For examples see Main Work, Vol. II, para.31–015.

(c) *Other Requirements*

No requirement of materiality

6–036   In *MCI Worldcom International Inc v Primus Telecommunications plc* [2004] EWCA Civ 957; [2004] All E.R. (D) 418 (Jul) Mance L.J., delivering the judgment of the court, said that this paragraph appears "to put the position too cautiously". As he saw the position, "whether there is a representation and what its nature is must be judged objectively according to the impact that whatever is said may be expected to have on a reasonable representee in the position and with the known characteristics of the actual representee . . . The position in the case of a fraudulent misrepresentation may of course be different" (at [30]).

[*Note 166: page* [450]]
The decision of the House of Lords in *Standard Chartered Bank v Pakistan National Shipping Corp (No.2)* is now reported at [2003] 1 A.C. 959.

3. DAMAGES FOR MISREPRESENTATION

Preliminary

6–041   [*Amend note 182, line 3: page* [452]]
The reference to Lord Tenterden's Act should be to "Statute of Frauds Amendment Act 1828."

(a) *Fraudulent Misrepresentation*

Contributory negligence

6–063   [*Note 257: page* [462]]
Standard Chartered Bank v Pakistan National Shipping Corp (No.2) is now reported at [2003] 1 A.C. 959.

(b) *Negligent Misrepresentation*

Misrepresentation Act, s.2(1)

6–067   An action under s.2(1) is not an action for negligence within the meaning of the Limitation Act 1980, s.14A, since it is not necessary for the claimant to aver any negligent act or omission: *Laws v Society of Lloyds* [2003] EWCA Civ 1887; *The Times*, January 23, 2004, at [91]. Whether it is an action in tort within s.2 of that Act was left open (see at [92]).

CHAPTER 7

DURESS AND UNDUE INFLUENCE

2. UNDUE INFLUENCE

(a) *Introduction*

Unconscionable conduct

[*Add to note 215: page* [536]]   **7–049**
   See also *Pesticcio v Huet* [2004] EWCA Civ 372; [2004] All E.R. (D) 36
(Apr), also a case of a gift.

(c) *Presumed Undue Influence*

(i) *Relationships giving rise to presumption of influence*

Guardian and ward

7–064   [*Correct note 315: page* [546]]
Kempson v Ashbee (1874) L.R. 10 Ch. App. 15

(iii) *A Transaction not explicable by Ordinary Motives*

Transaction not explicable by ordinary motives

7–073   [*Note 361: page* [552]]
Mortgage Agency Services Number Two Ltd v Chater is now reported at
[2004] 1 P. & C.R. 4.

(f) *Undue Influence by Third Party*

Transaction not on its face to the advantage of the surety

7–099   [*Note 456: page* [562]]
Mortgage Agency Services Number Two Ltd v Chater is now reported at
[2004] 1 P. & C.R. 4.

[*Add new paragraph, page* [565]]

7–106A   **Replacement mortgages.** Where a mortgage granted by a wife to a bank was
voidable against the bank because the bank had constructive notice of undue
influence by the husband, a replacement mortgage may also be voidable against
the bank even if when the replacement was given there was no undue influence,
at least where the replacement mortgage is taken as a condition of discharging the
original mortgage.[473a] It does not matter that the new agreement is a fresh
contract rather than a variation of the old one, provided that the replacement
mortgage is between the same parties.[473b] However, it seems that the replacement
mortgage must be inseparable from the original mortgage, in the sense that the
replacement mortgage was granted before the grantor became aware that she had
a right to avoid the original one and in order to discharge it.[473c]

[473a] *Yorkshire Bank plc v Tinsley* [2004] EWCA Civ 816; [2004] 3 All E.R. 463 at [19].
[473b] *Ibid.*, at [19]–[20].
[473c] *Ibid.*, at [24], [32] and [39].

Jointly-owned homes

7–108   [*Note 478: page* [566]]
First National Bank plc v Achampong is now reported at [2004] 1 F.C.R.
18.

Part Three

CAPACITY OF PARTIES

[N.B. THERE ARE NO AMENDMENTS TO CHAPTER 8]

CHAPTER 9

CORPORATIONS AND UNINCORPORATED ASSOCIATIONS

(d) *Registered Companies*

(i) *Contracts between Companies and Third Parties*

Ultra vires **and director's authority**

[*Replace last sentence of paragraph: page* [632]]   **9–031**
In *EIC Services Ltd v Phipps*[153] the Court of Appeal held that in the case of a bonus issue of shares, which is an internal corporate arrangement with no alteration in the assets of liabilities of the company, a shareholder could not be held as dealing with the company within the terms of s.35A.

[153] [2004] EWCA Civ 1069.

CHAPTER 10

THE CROWN, PUBLIC AUTHORITIES AND THE EUROPEAN COMMUNITY

[*Note 1: page* [663]]

Update reference to Wade and Forsyth, *Administrative Law* to (9th ed., 2004), Chaps 20 and 21.

1. THE CROWN: STATUS AND SPECIAL RULES

Fettering of discretion by contract

10–006   [*Note 35: page* [667]]

Delete reference to paras 10–007 *et seq.* and substitute para.10–017

Crown contracting through agents

10–009   [*Add to end of note 43: page* [668]]

Marubeni Hong Kong and South China Ltd v Government of Mongolia [2004] EWHC 472 (Comm); [2004] 2 Lloyd's Rep. 198.

2. The *Ultra Vires* Rule

Statutory Modification of *ultra vires* rule

[Add new paragraph: page [671]]   **10–015A**

Impact of human rights on *ultra vires* rule. Although an *ultra vires* agreement cannot be enforced against a public authority, the disappointed party may nonetheless be able to claim damages on the basis that the authority has violated his right to peaceful enjoyment of possessions.[70a] In *Stretch v United Kingdom*[70b] a local authority had granted the claimant a lease for 21 years, requiring the claimant to put up several industrial buildings, and containing an option to renew for a further 21 years. The option to renew was *ultra vires*. At the end of the term the claimant sought to exercise the option and the authority expressed a willingness to do so, but later changed its mind. It did not raise the *ultra vires* point until shortly before the trial began in the High Court. The European Court of Human Rights held that "in the circumstances of this case" the claimant had "a legitimate expectation of exercising the option to renew",[70c] and that this could be regarded as a possession. By refusing to grant the renewed lease or to offer any form of compensation, the authority had, it was held, interfered disproportionately with the claimant's right. Damages were not assessed on the basis that the claimant should be put in the position as if the renewal had been granted; rather, the court sought to identify what part of the initial consideration provided by the claimant was attributable to the option to renew, and ordered the authority to repay that amount. Although this decision is potentially of very wide application, it is submitted that its effect must not be overstated. The crucial question is what is required to give rise to a "legitimate expectation" of the promised benefit. On the narrowest reading of the judgment, twenty-one years' anticipation followed by the authority's apparent acquiescence would be needed. Certainly the case should not be seen as authority for the view that repudiation of any *ultra vires* agreement will always amount to a violation of protected human rights.

[70a] Art.1 of Protocol No.1, European Convention for the Protection of Human Rights and Fundamental Freedoms.
[70b] (2004) 38 E.H.R.R. 12.
[70c] *Ibid.*, at [35].

4. Estoppel and Legitimate Expectations

Estoppel and legitimate expectations

[Add to text after "contrary to statute", 7 lines from end: page [672]]   **10–017**

That there would be a substantive change is confirmed by a subsequent case, applying *Reprotech*, where it was observed that finding a legitimate expectation was "a task that is very different from an attempt to decide whether or not there is an estoppel in private law".[80a]

[80a] *R (on the application of Wandsworth LBC) v Secretary of State for Transport, Local Government and the Regions* [2003] EWHC 622 (Admin); [2004] 1 P. & C.R. 32 at [22].

10–017   [*Note 80: page* [672]]

Update references to *Wade and Forsyth* to (9th ed., 2004), pp.372–376, 500–505.

10–017   [*Add to text at end of paragraph*]

Where an authority is exercising the kind of public function that prevents it from being bound by an estoppel, it is also precluded from asserting an estoppel against an applicant.[81a]

> [81a] *Stancliffe Stone Co Ltd v Peak District National Park Authority* [2004] EWHC 1475 (QB); [2004] All E.R. (D) 232 at [35].

10–017   [*Page* [672]]

This paragraph must now be treated with caution in the light of recent cases applying the decision in *Regina (Reprotech (Pebsham) Ltd) v East Sussex County Council*.[81a] These cases have emphasised the planning law context of Lord Hoffmann's analysis, in particular that planning determinations concern the general public interest, bind the general public, and involve participation by other planning authorities, the Secretary of State and the general public itself.[81b] Many contracts made by public authorities will not share these features. Furthermore, in *Marubeni Hong Kong and South China Ltd v Government of Mongolia*,[81c] which concerned a commercial guarantee issued by the Mongolian Minister of Finance, counsel for the defendant cited *Reprotech* in support of an argument that the Minister's authority to issue the guarantee could not be determined using estoppel, but had to be analysed in terms of public law concepts.[81d] Cresswell J. rejected this submission, and proceeded to apply the orthodox principles of ostensible authority, which, as he acknowledged,[81e] is a species of estoppel.

> [81a] [2002] UKHL 8; [2003] 1 WLR 348.
> [81b] *R (on the application of Wandsworth LBC) v Secretary of State for Transport Local Government and the Regions* [2003] E.W.H.C. 622 (Admin); [2004] 1 P. & C.R. 32 at [10]–[13]; *Stancliffe Stone Co Ltd v Peak District National Park Authority* (Queen's Bench Division, June 22, 2004) at [32].
> [81c] [2004] EWHC 472 (Comm); [2004] 2 Lloyd's Rep. 198.
> [81d] *Ibid.*, at [97]–[102].
> [81e] *Ibid.*, at [124].

7. Public Procurement

Implied contract governing public tendering

10–025   [*Page* [675]]

This paragraph must now be read in the light of the Privy Council's decision in *Pratt Contractors Ltd v Transit New Zealand*,[115a] where it was conceded "in the light of modern authority"[115b] that submitting a tender in response to a request for tenders created a preliminary contract, which obliged the procuring authority to act fairly and in good faith in the selection process. This implied duty required any evaluation of the tenders to express honestly the views of the selectors. It also precluded selectors from taking steps to avoid receiving relevant information which they strongly suspected would show their opinion to be mistaken. However, there was no obligation on the procuring authority to eliminate any appearance of bias from the process, nor to avoid acting in other ways that, in different contexts, would be grounds for judicial review.[115c] Whether the same analysis will be adopted by English courts will depend on their willingness to follow the Commonwealth authorities establishing the implied duty; they may be reluctant to go as far one Australian decision, which saw the implied duty relating to tenders as part of a more general implied obligation of good faith.[115d]

[115a] [2003] UKPC 83; [2004] B.L.R. 143.
[115b] *Ibid.*, at [2]
[115c] *Ibid.*, at [47]
[115d] *Ibid.*, at [45]: "a somewhat controversial question".

EC Procurement Law

[Delete note 119: page [676] *and substitute]*   **10–026**
Directive 2004/18 on the co-ordination of procedures for the award of public works contracts, public supply contracts and public service contracts [2004] OJ L 134/114, supplemented by Directive 2004/17 co-ordinating the procurement procedures of entities operating in the water, energy, transport and postal services sectors [2004] OJ L 134/1. The previous Directives have been repealed (Directive 2004/18, art.82). Both Directives must be implemented by January 31, 2006.

[Add to last line of note 120, after "2001/2418) and": page [676]]
Public Contracts (Works, Services and Supply) and Utilities Contracts (Amendment) Regulations 2003

[Add to text at end of paragraph: page [677]]
These detailed express obligations concerning transparency of process may also give rise to a general implied obligation not to act in bad faith.[120a]

[120a] *Luck t/a Luck Arboricultural & Horticultural v London Borough of Tower Hamlets* [2003] EWCA Civ 52; [2003] 2 C.M.L.R. 12 at [59]–[60].

CHAPTER 11

POLITICAL IMMUNITY AND INCAPACITY

1. FOREIGN STATES, SOVEREIGNS, AMBASSADORS AND INTERNATIONAL ORGANISATIONS

Sovereign immunity and human rights

11–003   [Add at end of note 12: page [688]]
Voyiakis (2003) 52 I.C.L.Q. 297; Lloyd Jones (2003) 52 I.C.L.Q. 463.

State Immunity Act 1978

11–004   [Add to note 16: page [689]]
Military Affairs Office of the Embassy of the State of Kuwait v Caramba-Coker (E.A.T./1054/02/RN, April 10, 2003).

11–005   [Add in penultimate line of note 25: page [690]]
Al-Kadhimi v Government of Saudi Arabia [2003] EWCA Civ 1689.

[Add to note 26: page [690]]
cf. Military Affairs Office of the Embassy of the State of Kuwait v Caramba-Coker (E.A.T./1054/02/RN, April 10, 2003).

11–006   [Add at end of note 35: page [691]]
Norsk Hydro ASA v State Property Fund of Ukraine [2002] EWHC 2120 (Comm).

Acts of sovereign states

11–007   [Add at end of note 44: page [691]]
R. (on the Application of Abassi) v Secretary of State for Foreign and Commonwealth Affairs [2002] EWCA Civ 1598; [2003] U.K.H.R.R. 76.

[Add at end of note 45: page [691]]
Briggs (2002) 6 Sing. J. Int. & Comp. L. 953; Carruthers and Crawford (2003) 52 I.C.L.Q. 761.

Other persons entitled to immunity

[First line of note 103: page [697]]   **11–019**
Although immunity is conferred on the Commonwealth Secretariat, that immunity does not extend to the Commonwealth Secretariat Arbitration Tribunal, decisions of which may be reviewed under the Arbitration Act 1996: *Mohsin v Commonwealth Secretariat* [2002] EWHC 377 (Comm).

Part Four

THE TERMS OF THE CONTRACT

CHAPTER 12

EXPRESS TERMS

3. CONSTRUCTION OF TERMS

(d) *Effecting the intention of the parties*

Modifying

12–075   *[Add to note 305: page [743]]*
Contrast *Internaut Shipping GmbH v Fercometal SARL* [2003] EWCA Civ 812; [2003] 2 Lloyd's Rep. 430 (mistake beyond misnomer).

4. Admissibility of Extrinsic Evidence

(c) *Evidence as to the True Nature of the Agreement*

Evidence of Agency

[Add to note 488: page [762]]   **12–114**
See also *Internaut Shipping v Fercometal SARL* [2003] EWCA Civ 812;
[2003] 2 Lloyd's Rep. 430 (evidence of no agency).

(d) *Evidence to Interpret or Explain the Written Agreement*

Evidence of surrounding circumstances

[Add in line 7, after reference to Aqua Design & Play International Ltd v Kier   **12–119**
Regional Ltd in note 507: page [765]]
P&S Platt Ltd v Crouch [2003] EWCA Civ 1110; [2004] 1 P. & C.R. 18.

Subject-matter

[Add to note 530: page [767]]   **12–123**
cf. Compagnie Noga d'Importation et d'Exportation SA v Abacha (No. 4)
[2003] EWCA Civ 1100; [2003] 2 All E.R. (Comm.) 915 (where no intention to
conclude binding contract).

CHAPTER 13

IMPLIED TERMS

Intention of parties

13–004   [*Add to note 5: page* [774]]
cf. Kramer [2004] C.L.J. 384.

Efficacy to contract

13–005   [*Add to note 10: page* [775]]
CEL Group Ltd v Nedlloyd Lines UK Ltd [2003] EWCA Civ 1716; [2004] 1 Lloyd's Rep. 381 at [20]–[21].

Where term not implied

13–009   [*Add to note 39: page* [778]]
But in *Crossley v Faithful & Gould Holdings Ltd* [2004] EWCA Civ 293; [2004] I.R.L.R. 377, Morritt V.C. expressed the view that, in the case of a contract of employment, it was better to focus on questions of reasonableness, fairness and the balance of competing policy considerations rather than on the elusive concept of "necessity".

[*Add to note 42*]
Hadley Design Associates Ltd v Westminster City Council [2003] EWHC 1617; [2004] T.C.L.R. 1.

13–010   [*Page* [778]]
In *Interleasing (UK) Ltd v Morris* [2002] EWHC 1086 (Ch), where a contract made provision for obtaining counsel's opinion, no term was implied that the opinion would only be valid if given on the basis of true facts or proper instructions. In *Crossley v Faithful & Gould Holdings Ltd* [2004] EWCA Civ 293; [2004] I.R.L.R. 377, no term was implied into a contract of employment that an employer ought to take reasonable care of an employee's economic well-being by advising him of the financial consequences under an insurance scheme of his early retirement.

[*Add to note 48*]
But see the doubts expressed in *Crossley v Faithful & Gould Holdings Ltd*, above.

Prevention of performance

[Add after reference to Martin-Smith v Williams in note 69: page [780]]   **13-012**
  CEL Group Ltd v Nedlloyd Lines UK Ltd [2003] EWCA Civ 1716; [2004] 1
Lloyd's Rep. 381 at [11], [22] and [23].

Package travel etc

For the relationship between the Regulations and the (Athens) International   **13-034**
Convention on the Carriage of Passengers and their Luggage by Sea (see paras.
14–117 and 36–063, below), see *Lee v Airtours Holidays Ltd* [2004] 1 Lloyd's
Rep. 683.

EXEMPTION CLAUSES

2. RULES OF CONSTRUCTION

Burden of proof

14–018   *[Add at end of note 125: page* [805]*]*
followed in *Euro Cellular (Distribution) plc v Danzas Ltd* [2003] EWHC 3161 (Comm); [2004] 1 Lloyd's Rep. 521.

14–019   *[Add at end of note 127: page* [805]*]*
Euro Cellular (Distribution) plc v Danzas Ltd, above.

4. APPLICATION OF RULES TO PARTICULAR CONTRACTS

Misdelivery by carrier

14–033   *[Add at end of note 198: page* [814]*]*
East West Corporation v DKBS 1912 [2003] EWCA Civ 83; [2003] 3 W.L.R. 916 at [65]–[68].

5. Exemption Clauses and Third Parties

Bailment

[Add to note 274: page [824]]   **14–054**
East West Corporation v DKBS 1912 [2003] EWCA Civ 83; [2003] 3 W.L.R.
916 at [25]–[27].

[Add to note 279: page [825]]
East West Corporation v DKBS 1912, above, at [30], [69].

6. Statutory Control of Exemption Clauses

(a) *Unfair Contract Terms Act 1977*

Liability arising in contract

[Add to note 365: page [834]]   **14–072**
Hadley Design Associates Ltd v Westminster City Council [2003] EWHC
1617; [2004] T.C.L.R. 1.

[Add to note 377: page [835]]   **14–074**
Contrast *Hadley Design Associates Ltd v Westminster City Council*, above
(one month's termination clause in architects' contract not unreasonable).

(c) *Other Statutes*

Enterprise Act 2002

[Add to note 572: page [857]]   **14–131**
See SI 2003/1374, SI 2004/935.

[Add to note 575]
SI 2003/1375, SI 2004/935.

8. *Force Majeure* Clauses

Force majeure clauses

[Add to note 602: page [860]]   **14–137**
See Allen (2003) 147 S.J. 1416–1417.

"Prevented" clauses

14–141 *[Add to end of note 627: page* [864]]

Contrast *Mamidoil-Jetoil Greek Petroleum Co SA v Okta Crude Oil Refinery AD* [2003] 1 Lloyd's Rep. 1 (Comm Ct.); [2003] EWCA Civ 1031; [2003] 2 Lloyd's Rep. 635.

CHAPTER 15

UNFAIR TERMS IN CONSUMER CONTRACTS

2. The Unfair Terms In Consumer Contracts Regulations 1999

(a) *The Contracts Governed by the Regulations*

Contracts for the sale, etc. of an interest in land

[Pages [880]–[882]]

15–014—
15–017

Paragraphs 15–014—15–017 need to be read in the light of the decision of the Court of Appeal in *London Borough of Newham v Khatun* [2004] EWCA Civ 55; [2004] 3 W.L.R. 417. In that case, the question arose whether the 1993 Directive (and therefore the 1999 Regulations) applies to the terms on which accommodation is let by a local authority pursuant to its duty under the homeless persons legislation contained in Pt VII of the Housing Act 1996. Having looked at the *travaux préparatoires* of the Directive, the Court of Appeal noted the differences of terminology used by some of its different language versions to describe its subject matter (*e.g.* "seller of goods" and *"vendeur des biens"*, as identified in para.15–014 of the Main Text) and considered that these "effectively demolish" the textual argument that the English version's reference to "seller of goods" point to the exclusion of contracts relating to land: [2004] EWCA Civ 55, at

[78]–[83]. The Court of Appeal therefore held that the 1999 Regulations apply equally to contracts relating to land. Moreover, a few weeks after this decision, the European Court of Justice in *Freiburger Kommunalbauten GMbH Bauge-sellschaft & Co KG v Hofstetter* Case C-237/02 [2004] 2 C.M.L.R. 13 was apparently content to assume that a contract for the purchase of a building to be constructed falls within the ambit of the 1993 Directive, although the issue of the application of the 1993 Directive to contracts relating to land was not before the court.

"Sellers or suppliers"

15–021   *[Add to text after note 82: page* [884]]

In *London Borough of Newham v Khatun*[82a] the Court of Appeal held that the provision of accommodation by a local authority under a contract of tenancy, pursuant to its duty under the homeless persons legislation contained in Pt VII of the Housing Act 1996, falls within the scope of the 1993 Directive, as this activity comes within the words "trade, business or profession" under art.2(c) of the Directive, despite the statutory context of this provision.

[82a] [2004] EWCA Civ 55; [2004] 3 W.L.R. 417.

(b) *Contract Terms Governed by the Regulations*

[Add new paragraphs after paragraph 15–036: page [895]]

15–036A   **The relevance of construction of the contract.** In *Bairstow Eves London Central Ltd v Darlingtons*,[165a] the House of Lords' approach to reg.6(2) of the 1999 Regulations in the *First National Bank plc* case[165b] was applied to clauses setting the contract price in an estate agency contract. There a vendor of a flat (the "consumer") had entered a contract with an estate agent by which the latter undertook the sole agency to sell the flat on their behalf. Under its standard terms, the "standard commission" payable to the estate agent was set at 3 per cent of the sale price of the property, but "early payment" attracted a "discount rate" of 1.5 per cent of the sale price, early payment being defined as payment of the full sum payable within 10 working days of completion of the sale. It was further expressly specified that if such a full sum was not paid within this time, the "standard commission" would become payable together with interest at 3 per cent above base rate. After completing a sale, the vendor's solicitors did not pay the agent the *full* sum of the "discount rate" within the 10 day period (falling short by a mere £387) even though they were in funds to do so, and so the estate agent claimed the "standard rate" plus interest. It was then claimed that the terms of the contract setting the 3 per cent commission rate were unfair within the meaning of the 1999 Regulations, but to this the estate agents countered that these terms fell within the exclusion from the requirement of fairness contained in reg.6(2) of terms which relate to the "adequacy of the price or remuneration, as against the goods or services supplied in exchange."

15–036B   Having looked at the treatment of this provision by the House of Lords in the *First National Bank plc* case as described in para.15–036 of the Main Text, Gross

J. held that the applicability of reg.6(2) turned on an issue of construction of the contract, *viz* whether the agreement provided for a 3 per cent commission rate (or price) with the vendors having an option (but no obligation) to pay 1.5 per cent (in which case reg.6(2) *would* apply) or an obligation to pay a price of 1.5 per cent, with a "default" provision exercisable at the estate agents' option to insist on payment of 3 per cent (in which case reg.6(2) *would not* apply).[165c] In his view, the prevailing market, the pre-contractual negotiations between the parties, and their expectation that the 1.5 per cent commission would be paid within 10 days all indicated that *both* the parties to the contract contemplated an agreed operative price of 1.5 per cent with a default provision of 3 per cent.[165d] This view of the parties' intention was not precluded by the language used by the agreement as set in its contractual matrix, even though "at first blush" the reference to the higher price as the "standard commission rate" and the lower as the "early payment discounted rate" suggested the opposite conclusion[165e]: the idea that there was merely an option in the consumer (not an obligation) to pay the lower rate was "simply fanciful."[165f] As a result, reg.6(2) did not exclude this "default provision" from the requirement of fairness. Given that the view of the judge below that the clauses in question were unfair had not been appealed, the estate agent's claim to the higher commission rate failed.

[165a] [2004] EWHC 263; 2004 W.L. 1054905.
[165b] *Director General of Fair Trading v First National Bank plc* [2001] UKHL 52; [2002] 1 A.C. 481.
[165c] [2004] EWHC 263 at [26].
[165d] *Ibid.*, at [27].
[165e] *Ibid.*, at [29].
[165f] *Ibid.*, at [30].

(c) *The Requirement of Fairness*

(i) *The test of Unfairness*

[Add new paragraph after paragraph 15–047: page [903]]

The relative roles of the European Court of Justice and national courts. In   **15–048A**
Freiburger Kommunalbauten GmbH Baugesellschaft & Co KG v Hofstetter[207a] the European Court of Justice was asked by a national court to decide whether a clause in a particular consumer contract before it was unfair within the meaning of the 1993 Directive. This the European Court refused to do, noting that "in referring to concepts of good faith and significant imbalance between the rights and obligations of the parties, Article 3 of the [1993] Directive merely defines in a general way the factors that render unfair a contractual term that has not been individually negotiated."[207b] Given the range of factors which the Directive requires to be taken into account in assessing the fairness of a contract term, "the consequences of the term under the law applicable to the contract must also be taken into account. This requires that consideration be given to the national law."[207c] So, while the European Court "may interpret general criteria used by the Community legislation in order to define the concept of unfair terms, . . . it should not rule on the application of these general criteria to a particular term, which must be considered in the light of the particular circumstances of the case

in question."[207d] As a result, it is generally for a national court to decide whether a contract term satisfies the requirements for it to be regarded as unfair within the meaning of art.3(1) of the 1993 Directive.[207e]

[207a] Case C-237/02 of April 1, 2004 [2004] 2 C.M.L.R. 13.

[207b] *Ibid.*, at paras 19–21.

[207c] *Ibid.*, at para.21. For an example of this, see *Director General of Fair Trading plc v First National Bank plc* [2001] UKHL 52; [2002] 1 A.C. 481, discussed Main Text, para.15–061.

[207d] Case C-237/02 at para.22, "distinguishing" (at para.23) its earlier decision in *Océano Grupo Editorial SA v Murciano Quintero*, Joined Cases C-240/98 to C-244/98 of June 27, 2000 [2000] E.C.R. 1–4941, Main Text para.15–063, where it had held an internal territorial jurisdiction clause unfair on the basis that such a clause satisfied all the criteria necessary for it to be judged unfair for the purposes of the 1993 Directive without consideration of all the circumstances in which the contract was concluded or the advantages and disadvantages which the term would have under the applicable national law.

[207e] Case C-237/02, para.25.

(ii) *The "Indicative List" of terms*

Arbitration and adjudication clauses

15–072   [*Note 289: page* [917]]

Picardi v Cuniberti [2002] EWHC 2923 is reported at (2003) 19 Const. L.J. 350.

[*Add to text at end of paragraph: page* [917]]

On the other hand, in *Westminster Building Co Ltd v Beckingham*[291a] a private individual (the "consumer") who had commissioned a firm of builders to renovate his property under a contract falling outside the Housing Grants, Regeneration and Construction Act 1996 was held bound by an adjudication clause which it contained since this clause was not unfair in the circumstances: its terms were couched in plain and intelligible language and had been decided upon by the consumer's professional agents, chartered surveyors, who could have given him competent and objective advice as to its existence and effect.

[291a] [2004] EWHC 138 (TCC) esp. at [31]. See similarly *Lovell Projects Ltd v Legg* (TCC) [2003] B.L.R. 452.

Part Five

ILLEGALITY AND PUBLIC POLICY

CHAPTER 16

ILLEGALITY AND PUBLIC POLICY

2. The Position at Common Law

(a) Generally

Public policy

16–004   [*Add to note 12: page* [939]]
Kellar v Williams [2004] UKPC 30.

How illegality may affect a contract.

16–007   [*Add to text at end of paragraph: page* [942]]
The Law Commission has stated that "Generally, it seems that the commission of a legal wrong, or acting otherwise contrary to public policy, in the course of performing a contract does not, at common law, affect enforcement".[35a] Illegality will only preclude the enforcement of the contract where it has been "entered into with the purpose of doing [an] . . . unlawful or immoral act or the contract itself (as opposed to the mode of . . . performance) is prohibited by law."[35b]

[35a] *Illegal Transactions: The Effect Of Illegality On Contracts And Trusts* (LC CP No. 154, para.2.29) cited with approval in *Colen v Cebrian (U.K.) Ltd.* [2003] EWCA Civ 1676 at [44].
[35b] *Coral Leisure Group Ltd v Barnett* [1981] I.C.R. 503, 509.

(b) Objects which are Illegal by Common Law or Statute

Fraud

16–017   [*Add to the text at end of the paragraph: page* [949]]
However, where the contract in question is remote from the illegality, the court will enforce the contract.[92a]

[92a] *21st Century Logistic Solutions Ltd v Madysen Ltd* [2004] EWHC 231 (QB); [2004] 2 Lloyd's Rep. 92. (In this case a company that intended to evade the payment of VAT could nevertheless enforce a contract for the supply of goods, the avoidance of VAT not being an integral part of the contract.)

(c) Objects Injurious to good Government

(ii) Foreign affairs

Performance contrary to public policy in place for performance

16–028   [*Add to note 138: page* [953]]
Tekron Resources Ltd v Guinea Investment Co Ltd [2004] 2 Lloyd's Rep. 26

Illegality under foreign applicable law to contract

16–031   [*Add to note 149: page* [954]]
See also Mahonia Ltd v J.P. Morgan Chase Bank [2003] 2 Lloyd's Rep. 911; Mahonia Ltd v West LB AG [2004] EWHC 1938 (Comm).

(d) *Objects Injurious to the Proper Working of Justice*

(iv) *Maintenance and Champerty*

Public policy today respecting maintenance and champerty

[*Add at end of paragraph; page* [964]]   **16–049**
  In *Kellar v Williams*[237a] Lord Carswell stated *obiter* that the "content of public policy can change over the years, and it may now be time to reconsider the accepted [common law] prohibition [on conditional fees] in the light of modern practising conditions"[237b]

[237a] [2004] UKPC 30.
[237b] *ibid.*, at [21].

Non-champertous agreements between solicitor and client

[*Replace note 295: page* [968]]   **16–056**
  [295] *ibid.*, s.58(3). Various statutory instruments have been made with respect to conditional fee orders: see *Sharratt v London Central Bus Co Ltd* [2003] EWCA Civ 718; [2003] 4 All E.R. 590 where the law is fully analysed.

(f) *Contracts in Restraint of Trade*

(i) *Scope of the doctrine*

Criteria for application of doctrine

[*Add at end of paragraph: page* [984]]   **16–083**
However, the absence of reciprocal obligation may be a factor in determining whether a restraint is reasonable.[447a]

  [447a] *Societa Explosivi Industriali SpA v Ordnance Technologies (U.K.) Ltd* [2004] EWHC 48 (Ch), at [145].

Legitimate interests of the parties.

[*Add to note 481: page* [988]]   **16–092**
  Countryside Assured Financial Services Ltd v Deanne Smart [2004] EWHC 1214.

(ii) *Employer and Employee*

Trade secrets and connection with customers

[*Add to note 577: page* [999]]   **16–107**
  Fibrenetix Storage Ltd v Davis [2004] EWHC 1359 (QB) (protection of pricing policies).

(iv) *Partners*

Analogous Agreements

16–119   [*Add to text at end of paragraph: page* [1010]]
In *Buchanan v Alba Diagnostics Ltd*[680a] Lord Hoffmann upheld as valid a perpetual restraint in the assignment of a patent entitling the assignee to the rights of any improvement in the patent. He considered that it was in the public interest for inventors to be able to borrow money on the security of future rights,[680b] and a clear implication of his reasoning is that the agreement was treated as being analogous to the sale of the goodwill of a business.

[680a] [2004] UKHL 5; 2004 S.C.(H.L.) 9.
[680b] *ibid.*, at [29].

(v) *Supply and Acquisition of Goods: Restraints in Vertical Agreements*

Application of doctrine

16–120   [*Add to note 681 at end: page* [1010]]
The court held in *Days Medical Aids Ltd v Pihsiang Machinery Co Ltd* [2004] EWHC 44 (Comm) that an agreement not invalidated by Art.81 of the EU Treaty could not be subject to the common law restraint of trade doctrine.

3. CONTRACTS UNENFORCEABLE BY STATUTE

(a) *General principles*

Statute: one party only affected

16–153   [*Add to note 798: page* [1026]]
Crehan v Inntrepreneur Pub Company CPC [2004] EWCA Civ 637; [2004] E.C.C. 28, the claimant, as a matter of Community Law, could claim damages from his co-contractor with respect to an agreement which breached Art.81 of the EU Treaty. The claimant in *Crehan* was not significantly responsible for any distortion of competition.

4. ENFORCEMENT OF COLLATERAL AND PROPRIETARY RIGHTS

(a) *The Maxim Ex Turpi Causa Non Oritur Actio and Related Rules*

Tainting

16–161   [*Delete note 825 and replace: page* [1030]]
    [825] *Vakante v Addey & Stanhope School* [2004] EWCA Civ 1065 where the Court of Appeal (Civil Division) upheld the decision of the Employment Appeal Tribunal that illegality precluded the claimant from pursuing his racial discrimination claim. See also *Wheeler v Quality Deep Ltd* [2004] EWCA Civ 1085 where the lack of English and limited knowledge of tax and national insurance provisions were considered relevant in determining the extent to which the employee participated in an illegality.

(c) *Recovery of Money Paid or Property Transferred under Illegal Contracts*

Transfer of property under illegal transaction

[*Add to note 901: page* [1039]] **16–172**
The court will not enforce a claim by a person claiming funds held by a person
in the position of trustee (in this case a solicitor) where the claimant has to rely
on his fraud: see *Halley v Law Society* [2003] EWCA Civ 97.

Determination of limited interests created by illegal transactions

[*Note 904: page* [1040]] **16–173**
Update the reference to *Treitel* to (11th ed., 2003), p.496.

[*Note 914: page* [1041] **16–174**
Update reference to *Treitel* to (11th ed., 2003), p.496.

[*Note 916: page* [1041]]
Update reference to *Treitel, op. cit.*, at p.496.

[*Add at end of paragraph: page* [1042]] **16–175**
Although collateral rights, as in *Tinsley v Milligan*[919a], may arise out of an
illegal contract, a collateral right normally involves a proprietary right and does
not include a right of action on the contract itself.[919b]

[919a] *ibid.*
[919b] *Mahonia Ltd v J P Morgan Chase Bank* [2003] 2 Lloyd's Rep. 911, at [27]. See also *Mahonia
Ltd v West LB AG* [2004] EWHC 1938 (Comm).

Oppression and fraud

[*Note 942: page* [1045]] **16–180**
Update reference to *Treitel* to (11th ed., 2003), pp.492–493.

Mistake

[*Note 943: page* [1045]] **16–181**
Update reference to *Treitel, op. cit.*, at p.493.

6. PLEADING AND PRACTICE

Pleading of illegality

[*Add at end of note 1029: page* [1055]] **16–199**
Bim Kemi AB v Blackburn Chemicals Ltd [2004] EWHC 166 (Comm) (court
could take notice that agreement was illegal under Art.81 of the EU Treaty).

Part Six

JOINT OBLIGATIONS, THIRD PARTIES AND ASSIGNMENT

[N.B. THERE ARE NO AMENDMENTS TO CHAPTER 17]

CHAPTER 18

THIRD PARTIES

2. THE COMMON LAW DOCTRINE

(a) *Parties to the Agreement*

Collateral contracts

18–005   [*Add to note 24: page* [1076]]

Morin v Bonhams & Brooks Ltd has been affirmed on the ground that the governing law was that of Monaco: [2003] EWCA Civ 1802; [2004] 1 All E.R. (Comm.) 880.

[*Add to text at end of paragraph: page* [1077]]

Similarly, in *Brook Street Bureau v Dacas*[31a] an employment agency entered into contracts with workers whom it supplied to a local authority. It was held that there was not only an express contract between the workers and the agency, but also an implied contract between the workers and the authority.

[31a] [2004] EWCA Civ 217; [2004] I.R.L.R. 358.

Agency

[*Add to note 60: page* [1080]]   **18–012**
Vitesse Yacht Charterers SL v Spiers (The Deverne II) [2003] EWHC 2426 (Admlty); [2004] 1 Lloyd's Rep. 179 (contract to charter yacht for holiday to be taken by two persons together made by one of them on behalf of both).

3. Scope

(a) *Liability in Negligence to Third Parties*

Duty of care may be owed to third party

[*Add to note 117, line 6: page* [1087]]   **18–022**
Niru Battery Manufacturing Co v Milestone Trading Ltd [2003] EWCA Civ 1446 is now reported in [2004] 1 Lloyd's Rep. 344.

4. Contracts For The Benefit Of Third Parties

(a) *Effects of a Contract for the Benefit of a Third Party*

(i) *Promisee's Remedies*

Damages in respect of third party's loss: exceptions in general

[*Add to note 269: page* [1109]]   **18–050**
In *Rolls Royce Power Engineering plc v Ricardo Consulting Engineers Ltd* [2003] EWHC 2871 (T.C.C.); [2004] 2 All E.R. (Comm.) 129 it was held that a contracting party could not recover damages in respect of a third party's loss as trustee for the third party where the other contracting party at the time of the contract did not know or have reason to know that the former party was contracting as trustee.

[*Add to note 272, line 10, after reference to [1977] C.L.J. 24: page* [1110]]
In the *Rolls Royce Power* case, above, n.269, it was held that the "rule in *Dunlop v Lambert*" ((1839) 2 Cl. & F. 626, 627) applied only if at the time of the contract it was "in the actual contemplation of the parties that an identified third party or a third party who was a member of an identified class might suffer damage in the event of a breach of the contract" (at [124]).

Scope of the "broader ground"

18–059   [*Add to note 324: page* [1116]]

In *Rolls Royce Power Engineering plc v Ricardo Consulting Engineers Ltd*
[2003] EWHC 2871 (TCC); [2004] 2 All E.R. (Comm.) 129, Judge Seymour
Q.C. said (at [128]) that the "broader ground" for the decision in the *Linden
Gardens* case ([1994] 1 A.C. 85) was not easy to apply "where the alleged
damage is damage to, or failure to repair, property and there is no suggestion of
consequential loss."

(b) *Exceptions to the Doctrine*

(iii) *Other Statutory Exceptions*

Third parties' rights against insurers

18–123   [*Note 615, line 14: page* [1153]]

In *Centre Reinsurance International Co v Curzon International Ltd* [2004]
EWHC 200 (Ch); [2004] 2 All E.R. (Comm.) 28 it was held that a transfer of
rights under the Third Parties (Rights against Insurers) Act 1930 could occur
"notwithstanding that the insured's liability to the third party has yet to be
established" (at [29]). The contrary view in *Nigel Upchurch Associates v
Aldridge Estates Investment Co Ltd* [1993] 1 Lloyd's Rep. 533 (cited in Main
Work, p.1153, n.615) was rejected.

5. Enforcement Against Third Parties

Lack of causal connection

18–134   [*Add to note 667: page* [1160]]

The mortgagee of a ship is not obliged to defer the exercise of his power of
sale under the mortgage even though such exercise interferes with contracts made
by the mortgagor for the carriage of goods in the ship with the shippers of those
goods: *Den Norske Bank ASA v Acemex Management Co* [2003] EWCA Civ
1559; [2004] All E.R. (Comm.) 904, at [22].

ASSIGNMENT

1. ASSIGNMENT

(b) *Equitable Assignments*

Formalities for equitable assignments

[Add to note 98; page [1173]]   **19–025**

In *Coulter v Chief of Dorset Police* [2003] EWHC 3391 (Ch); [2004] 1 W.L.R. 1425 it was held that the benefit of a judgment (for costs) had been assigned in equity by a retiring chief constable to his successor. Patten J., after referring to the need for there to be "a sufficient expression of an intention to assign" for an equitable assignment, said (at [16]): "What, in my judgment, acts as the trigger, if trigger is needed, is the manifest event of the resignation or retirement of the existing office holder, and the assumption of office by his successor. That is, as I see it, a sufficient outward manifestation of an intention that the successor office holder should obtain the benefits held on trust by a predecessor, for there to be an equitable assignment of the benefit of the judgment."

(c) *Principles Applicable to Statutory and Equitable Assignments*

(i) *What Rights are Assignable*

Rights declared by contract to be incapable of assignment

19–043 [*Add to note 159; page* [1182]]
Thomas, "Contractual Intention and the Nature of Leases" (2004) 120 L.Q.R. 222

[N.B. THERE ARE NO AMENDMENTS TO CHAPTER 20]

Part Seven

PERFORMANCE AND DISCHARGE

CHAPTER 21

PERFORMANCE

2. TIME OF PERFORMANCE

Time made expressly or implicitly "of the essence"

21–013

[Add to note 82: page [1241]]
Re Simoco Digital UK Ltd: Thunderbird Industries LLC v Simoco Digital UK Ltd [2004] EWHC 209 (Ch); [2004] 1 B.C.L.C. 541 at [14].

Consequences of time being "of the essence"

21–015

[Add to note 101: page [1243]]
State Securities plc v Initial Industry Ltd [2004] All E.R. (D) 317 (Jan).

4. PAYMENT

(b) *Appropriation of Payments*

Creditor's right to appropriate

21–061

[In note 344, insert after reference to Lowther v Heaver: page [1267]]
Potomek Construction Ltd v Zurich Securities Ltd [2003] EWHC 2827 (Ch); [2004] 1 All E.R. (Comm.) 672 at [69].

[49]

Appropriation as between principal and interest

21–067   *[Add to note 364: page* [1270]]
Potomek Construction Ltd v Zurich Securities Ltd [2003] EWHC 2827 (Ch);
[2004] 1 All E.R. (Comm.) 672 at [69].

CHAPTER 22

DISCHARGE BY AGREEMENT

3. ACCORD AND SATISFACTION

Ineffective accord

[Add to note 75, at end: page [1292]*]*   **22–021**
This is likely to be a difficult hurdle to overcome (see, for example, *Champion Investments Ltd v Ahmed* [2004] All E.R. (D) 28 (Aug)). In the rare case in which it is overcome, compromise may be vitiated by a mistake of law as well as a mistake of fact: *Brennan v Bolt Burden (a firm)* [2004] EWCA Civ 1017; [2004] 1 All E.R. (D) 551 (Jul) at [17].

6. WAIVER

[Insert new paragraph: page [1303]*]*
Contracting out of waiver. It would appear that there is no general principle   **22–044A**
of law that parties to a contract cannot restrict the operation of the doctrine of waiver by the terms of their contract.[182a] In *State Securities plc v Initial Industry Ltd*[182b] Jonathan Gaunt Q.C., sitting as a Deputy Judge of the High Court, stated,

> "I can, however, see no reason in principle why the parties to an equipment lease . . . or other commercial contract, should not be free to stipulate that a particular act, such as payment of a rental instalment should not be taken to waive a right to terminate for an earlier breach. After all, such a provision may be very convenient and operate to the benefit of both parties. The finance company may want to encourage the lessee

to correct the breach but not want him to fall behind with his payments while he does so. It may be in the interests of the lessee that the finance company should not have to take an early decision whether to terminate." [182c]

However it cannot be assumed that the courts in all cases will give effect to a term of the contract which purports to exclude or limit the operation of the doctrine of waiver; in some circumstances the term of the contract may not suffice to deny effect to a clear and unequivocal representation made by one party to the contract. [182d]

[182a] *State Securities plc v Initial Industry Ltd* [2004] All E.R. (D) 317 (Jan).
[182b] [2004] All E.R. (D) 317 (Jan).
[182c] At [57].
[182d] *I-Way Ltd v World Online Telecom Ltd* [2002] EWCA Civ 413 (Court of Appeal refused to give summary judgment in a case in which the court was asked, in effect, to enforce a term of the contract which provided that "no addition, amendment or modification of this Agreement shall be effective unless it is in writing and signed by or on behalf of both parties.")

CHAPTER 23

DISCHARGE BY FRUSTRATION

1. INTRODUCTION

Introduction

[*Note 1: page* [1311]]   **23–001**
Update reference to Treitel, *Frustration and Force Majeure* to (2nd. ed., 2004).

Historical Introduction

[*Note 10: page* [1312]]   **23–004**
Update reference to Treitel to (2nd. ed., 2004), Chap.2.

2. THE TEST FOR FRUSTRATION

[*Note 24: page* [1314]]
Update reference to Treitel, *Frustration and Force Majeure* to (2nd. ed., 2004), paras 16–006—16–016.

Practical differences between the tests

23–018 *[Note 76: page* [1321]]
Update reference to Treitel, *Frustration and Force Majeure* to (2nd. ed., 2004), paras 16–013—16–016.

3. ILLUSTRATIONS OF THE DOCTRINE

(b) *Common Types of Frustrating Events*

(i) *Subsequent Legal Changes and Supervening Illegality*

Changes affecting employment

23–022 *[Note 104: page* [1324]]
Update reference to Treitel to (2nd. ed., 2004), Chap.8.

(ii) *Cancellation of an Expected Event*

The "coronation cases"

23–032 *[Note 130: page* [1327]]
Update reference to Treitel to (2nd. ed., 2004), paras 7–006—7–014.

(iii) *Delay*

Delay

23–034 *[Note 142: page* [1329]]
Update reference to Treitel to (2nd. ed., 2004), paras 5–036—5–056.

(c) *Application of the Doctrine to Common Types of Contracts*

(i) *Personal Contracts*

Death

23–036 *[Note 162: page* [1330]
Update reference to Treitel to (2nd. ed., 2004), para.2–015.

Illness or incapacity

23–037 *[Add to Note 168: page* [1331]]
It may be that permanent incapacity alone will not suffice to frustrate a contract of employment, on the basis that the contract itself may, exceptionally, envisage the possibility that the employee will continue to be employed notwithstanding the fact that he or she is suffering a permanent incapacity: see *R (Verner) v Derby City Council* [2003] EWHC 2708 (Admin); [2004] I.C.R. 535 at [66]. Lindsay J. concluded (at [68]) that in such a case the contract of employment

continues to exist "in an entirely shadowy form in which, by reason of the employee's incapacity and retirement, the employer cannot require any performance and the employee cannot offer it."

(ii) *Charterparties*

[Note 184: page [1333]]
Update reference to Treitel to (2nd. ed., 2004), paras 5–052—5–054.

(v) *Leases and Tenancies*

[Note 220: page [1339]]
Update reference to Treitel to (2nd. ed., 2004), Chap.11.

Prohibition on intended use

[Note 234: page 1340]]   **23–052**
Update reference to Treitel to (2nd. ed., 2004), paras 7–023—7–0024 and 11–022.

4. THE LIMITS OF FRUSTRATION

Express provision

[Note 253: page [1343]]   **23–056**
Update reference to Treitel to (2nd. ed., 2004), Chap.12.

[Add to the end of Note 254]
cf. *R (Verner) v Derby City Council* [2003] EWHC 2708 (Admin); [2004] I.C.R. 535 at [66].

Significance of a foreseen event

[Note 264: page [1344]]   **23–057**
Update reference to Treitel, *Frustration and Force Majeure* to (2nd. ed., 2004), Chap.13.

Event foreseeable but not foreseen

[Note 273: page [1345]]   **23–058**
Update reference to Treitel to (2nd. ed., 2004), para.13–012.

Self-induced frustration

[Note 274: page [1345]]   **23–059**
Update reference to Treitel to (2nd. ed., 2004), Chap.14.

Partial excuse at common law

23–066   [*Note 311: page* [1350]]
Update reference to Treitel, *Frustration and Force Majeure* to (2nd. ed., 2004), para.5–060.

5. The Legal Consequences of Frustration

23–068   [*Note 318: page* [1351]]
Update reference to Treitel to (2nd. ed., 2004), Chap.15.

Law Reform (Frustrated Contracts) Act 1943

23–072   [*Note 329: page* [1353]]
Update reference to Treitel to (2nd. ed., 2004), paras 15–049—15–096.

CHAPTER 24

DISCHARGE BY BREACH

1. IN GENERAL

Affirmation

[*Add to note 19: page* [1368]]   **24–003**
State Securities plc v Initial Industry Ltd [2004] All E.R. (D) 317 (Jan) (acceptance of rental payment held not to have amounted to an election to continue with the contract).

Acceptance of repudiation

[*Add to note 91: page* [1377]]   **24–013**
When deciding whether or not inconsistent actions amount to an acceptance of a repudiation, the courts apply an objective test: *Enfield London Borough Council v Sivanandan* [2004] EWHC 672 (QB); [2004] All E.R. (D) 73 (April) at [38]–[39].

[*Add to note 95*]
In such a case the contractor may be absolved from his contractual obligation before he communicates his acceptance: *Potter v RJ Temple* [2003] All E.R. (D) 327 (Dec.)

3. Impossibility Created by One Party

Anticipatory breach

24–030   *[Add to note 174 after [1957] 2 Q.B. 401, 449–450: page [1389]]*
Re Simoco Digital UK Ltd: Thunderbird Industries LLC v Simoco Digital UK Ltd [2004] EWHC 209 (Ch); [2004] 1 B.C.L.C. 541 at [22]–[23].

5. Consequences of Discharge

Effect on contract

24–048   *[Add to note 258: page [1399]]*
Similarly, an adjudication provision in a contract will survive the discharge of the contract: *Connex South Eastern Ltd v MJ Building Services Group plc* [2004] EWHC 1518 (TCC) at [25].

CHAPTER 25

OTHER MODES OF DISCHARGE

2. ALTERATION OR CANCELLATION OF A WRITTEN INSTRUMENT

Material alteration

[Insert new note 111a after "alteration" at the beginning of line 12: page [1417]   **25–020**
[111a] It may be necessary in certain cases to distinguish between an "alteration" to a document and an "appendage" to the contract. Thus the addition of an incorrect date after the document has been signed may amount to an "appendage" rather than an alteration: *Moussavi-Azad v Sky Properties Ltd* [2003] EWHC 2669 (QB); [2003] All E.R. (D) 38 (Dec) at [49]. This may be thought to introduce an unnecessary element of sophistry into the rule and that the better view is that such an addition is an "alteration" and the vital question then becomes whether that alteration is "material".

Immaterial alteration

[Add to note 128: page [1418]]   **25–023**
Moussavi-Azad v Sky Properties Ltd [2003] EWHC 2669 (QB); [2003] All E.R. (D) 38 (Dec) at [48]–[51].

Part Eight

REMEDIES FOR BREACH OF CONTRACT

CHAPTER 26

DAMAGES

1. NATURE AND KINDS OF DAMAGES

(g) *Exemplary Damages and Depriving the Defendant of his Profit*

Partial disgorgement on the *Wrotham Park* basis

26–024   [*Add to note 139 at end: page* [1437]]

A substantial level of damages has been awarded on the *Wrotham Park* basis: *Lane v O'Brien Homes* [2004] EWHC 303 (QB). The claimant had lost "the value of [her] bargaining position"; damages of £150,000 were awarded against a builder whose profit was at least £280,000 (case noted by Campbell, (2004) 67 M.L.R. 817). See also *Gafford v Graham* (1999) 77 P. & C.R. 73; *Amec Developments Ltd v Jury's Hotel Management (UK) Ltd* [2001] 1 E.G.L.R. 81

3. REMOTENESS OF DAMAGE

(d) *Expenditure Wasted or Incurred as a Result of the Breach*

Damages assessed on a "no transaction" basis

[*Add to note 383: page* [1466]]   **26–070**
(followed in *Hok Sport Ltd v Aintree Racecourse Co Ltd* [2002] EWHC 3094; [2003] Lloyd's Rep. P.N. 148).

(e) *Non-pecuniary Losses*

Mental Distress and Disappointment: nervous shock

[*Add to note 409 after the reference to Malik's case: page* [1468]]   **26–074**
In *Eastwood v Magnox Electric plc* [2004] UKHL 35; [2004] 3 W.L.R. 322, Lord Nicholls said (at [11]) that if the facts of *Addis* occurred today, the claimant would have a remedy at common law for breach of contract: see para.26–077, below.

[*Add to note 412*]
On *Johnson v Unisys*, see the text added to para.26–077, below.

[*Add to text after note 417: page* [1469]]
Damages for breach of contract may be awarded to a mother for the mental distress caused by the loss of the company of her child.[417a]

[417a] *Hamilton-Jones v David & Snape* (a firm) [2003] EWHC 3147 (Ch); [2004] 1 W.L.R. 924 (solicitor's failure allowed father to remove children from the UK).

[*Add to note 419: page* [1469]]
Barber v Somerset County Council [2004] UKHL 13; [2004] 1 W.L.R. 1089 (employee's psychiatric injury caused by work-related stress).

Loss of reputation

[*Add to text at the end of the paragraph: page* [1470]]   **26–077**
But this case has later been distinguished by the House of Lords, which held that an employee may have a common law claim for financial loss where his employer has acted unfairly towards him prior to, and independently of, his subsequent unfair dismissal.[430a] However, it should be noted that in another case the House of Lords held that in his unfair dismissal claim an employee cannot recover compensation for non-economic or non-pecuniary loss, such as distress, humiliation or loss of reputation.[430b]

[430a] *Eastwood v Magnox Electric plc* [2004] UKHL 35; [2004] 3 W.L.R. 322.
[430b] *Dunnachie v Kingston upon Hull City Council* [2004] UKHL 36; [2004] 3 W.L.R. 310 (interpreting s.123 of the Employment Rights Act 1996).

5. MITIGATION OF DAMAGE

"Reasonable steps"

26–095   [*Add to note 518: page* [1480]]
See also paras 26–095A—26–095D below.

[*After paragraph 26–095, add new paragraphs: page* [1481]]

26–095A   **Impecuniosity of the claimant.** A recent tort case in the House of Lords leads to the question whether the impecuniosity of the claimant could be relevant in a contractual claim. In *Lagden v O'Connor*[523a] the House of Lords held that it would not follow the dicta in *The Liesbosch* case[523b] to the effect that the plaintiff's impecuniosity was not relevant to the assessment of damages. *Lagden v O'Connor* was a claim in tort where the claimant's car had been damaged by the defendant's negligence. Since the claimant could not afford simply to hire a replacement car while his was being repaired (the car-hire firm would require him to make an up-front payment) he entered into a more expensive hire arrangement with an "accident hire" insurance company under which he need not pay anything in advance. The majority of their Lordships held that it was reasonably foreseeable that an impecunious claimant might reasonably incur the higher cost of credit hire because he had no other choice in obtaining a replacement car. Thus the claimant's foreseeable impecuniosity resulted in his entitlement to higher damages in tort than would have been awarded to others who could afford to pay for ordinary hire. This rule "requires the wrongdoer to bear the consequences if it was reasonably foreseeable that the injured party would have to borrow money or incur some other kind of expenditure to mitigate his damages".[523c] This language ("wrongdoer", "injured party") is not appropriate to a claim in contract where the main remoteness rule (the first rule in *Hadley v Baxendale*) is different from that in tort: the kind of loss within the reasonable contemplation of the parties at the time of making the contract.[523d] But even in contract the claimant's impecuniosity might be relevant if it prevented him from choosing a cheaper form of mitigation. The rules on mitigation and those on remoteness are entwined in some cases, where what was "within reasonable contemplation" and what was "reasonable" mitigation are treated as interchangeable concepts. In the *Monarch S.S.* case,[523e] Lord Wright said (with reference to the decision of the House of Lords in *Muhammad Issa el Sheikh Ahmad v Ali*[523f]) that "damages consequent on impecuniosity were held not too remote because . . . the loss was such as might reasonably be expected to be in the contemplation of the parties as likely to flow from breach of the obligation undertaken".[523g] This means that the claimant's impecuniosity will be relevant in contract if it falls within the defendant's reasonable contemplation (as at the time of contracting) as not unlikely to affect the claimant's ability to mitigate after a breach of the particular undertaking, *viz.*, that the claimant would be likely to incur greater than usual expense (or higher than normal interest charges) in a reasonable attempt to mitigate. This test will not be easy for the claimant to satisfy if he cannot prove that the defendant actually knew of his impecuniosity (which is the situation examined in the next paragraph.) Thus, there is no reported case holding his impecuniosity to be relevant in relation to the market price rule in the sale of goods[523h] or to the similar market price rule for breach of a contract of hire.[523i]

Actual knowledge of the claimant's impecuniosity. The claimant's impecu- 26–095B
niosity will be relevant in contract if the second rule in *Hadley v Baxendale* is satisfied *viz.*, if, at the time of contracting, the contract-breaker had actual knowledge of special circumstances under which a breach was likely to cause the claimant greater or different loss from that to be normally expected under normal circumstances.[523j] The claimant's impecuniosity could be a "special circumstance" under this rule if, with his knowledge of it, the defendant could foresee that the claimant could mitigate his loss caused by the breach only by incurring greater expense than would be incurred by a financially secure person. The claimant must act "reasonably" in his mitigating actions but what is reasonable for a claimant known to be impecunious may be different from the case of a person with financial resources.[523k] One of the mitigation rules is that the claimant is entitled to damages for any loss or expense incurred by him in reasonably attempting to mitigate his loss, even where this attempt was unsuccessful or led to greater loss.[523l]

Several cases illustrate the position.[523m] In *Wadsworth v Lydall*,[523n] on the 26–095C
dissolution of a farming partnership between the parties, the defendant was obliged to pay £10,000 to the plaintiff on a fixed date. The defendant knew that the plaintiff needed another farm and would be dependent on payment of that sum on that date to finance any purchase. When the defendant failed to pay, the Court of Appeal awarded the plaintiff as special damages the extra interest charges and legal costs incurred by him as a result of the breach.[523o] In *Bacon v Cooper*[523p] the rotor of the plaintiff's machine was damaged beyond repair as a result of the defendant's breach of contract. The only available replacement cost £41,500 which the plaintiff, a dealer in scrap metal, could not finance out of his own resources. It was held that the plaintiff had acted reasonably in obtaining it on hire purchase at a high rate of interest.[523q] A further authority is *Trans Trust S.P.R.L. v Danubian Trading Co Ltd*.[523r] The buyers undertook that a confirmed credit was to be opened forthwith in favour of the firm from which the sellers were obtaining the goods. The buyers knew that the sellers were not in a position themselves to open the necessary credit. The Court of Appeal held that the loss due to this impecuniosity of the sellers was not too remote because it was within the reasonable contemplation of the parties as likely to flow from the buyer's breach of contract in failing to obtain the credit.

Another case appears to accept the principle but it was found on the facts that 26–095D
the defendants did not know of the plaintiff's special financial arrangements. In *Compania Financiera "Soleada" S.A. v Hamoor Tanker Corporation Inc.*[523s] the plaintiff's vessel was arrested in breach of contract: since it was reasonably foreseeable that the plaintiff would seek to obtain its release and for that purpose

would obtain a guarantee for payment of the debt, the Court of Appeal held that the expense in doing so, if reasonable, would be recoverable either because it was within the remoteness rules, or as the expense of reasonable mitigation.[523t] But because the particular financial arrangements between the plaintiffs and their bank were not known to the defendants, the high interest charges actually incurred by the plaintiffs were held to be "wholly unreasonable" and so not recoverable.

[523a] [2003] UKHL 64; [2004] 1 A.C. 1067.
[523b] [1933] AC 449, 460.
[523c] per Lord Hope, at [61].
[523d] See paras 26–045—26–051.
[523e] [1949] A.C. 196.
[523f] [1947] A.C. 427.
[523g] [1949] A.C. 196, 224; see para.26–056, n.295.
[523h] See paras 26–097, 43–415.
[523i] See para.26–097, n.530.
[523j] See paras 26–054—26–056.
[523k] On the question of actual knowledge, see para.26–089, text at n.495.
[523l] See para.26–105.
[523m] See also para.26–097 below.
[523n] [1981] 1 W.L.R. 598.
[523o] See para.26–089: the House of Lords approved the decision, ibid., n.490.
[523p] [1982] 1 All E.R. 397; see also para.26–145)
[523q] The case was not explicitly put on the ground of the second rule in Hadley v Baxendale but on the reasonableness of mitigation, as was Robbins of Putney Ltd v Meek [1971] R.T.R. 345 (see para.26–097, below.)
[523r] [1952] 2 Q.B. 297.
[523s] [1981] 1 W.L.R. 274.
[523t] Although Lord Denning preferred the former, his colleagues seemed to use the two concepts interchangeably.

Sale of goods

26–097 [Add to text at the end of the paragraph: page [1482]]
The relevance of the claimant's impecuniosity is discussed above.[532a] The market price rule is fundamental to the sale of goods: if the seller fails to deliver, the buyer's damages are prima facie the difference between the contract price and the market price at the date of breach.[532b] The rule assumes that the buyer should be able to finance the purchase of substitute goods at the time of the breach, even though he may not receive the damages until much later. The rule works reasonably well if he retains the balance of the price and there has not been a substantial rise in the market price. But the buyer's lack of financial resources could prevent his purchase of a substitute if he had paid the price (or a substantial deposit) in advance, or if the rise in price has been substantial. But to date none of these factors has prevented the application of the prima facie rule.[532c] Actual knowledge of the buyer's lack of resources has been treated as relevant to the purchase of a house[532d]; and the seller's decision to re-sell quickly because he was short of liquid resources was held to be reasonable mitigation in Robbins of Putney Ltd v Meek [1971] R.T.R. 345 (sale of goods).

[532a] This Supplement, paras 26–095A—26–095D above.
[532b] See Vol.II, para.43–415.

532c See Benjamin's *Sale of Goods* (6th ed.) §17–008. On the *prima facie* nature of the rule, see Vol.II, 43–416.
532d *Wroth v Tyler* [1974] Ch. 30: see this Supplement, para.26–098A below.

[*After paragraph 26–098, add new paragraph: page* [1482]]

Sale of land. In *Wroth v Tyler*536a the contract-breaker's knowledge of the   **26–098A**
plaintiffs' lack of resources was treated as relevant to their ability to mitigate.536b
Both the seller and the purchasers of a house contemplated at the date of the
contract that there would be a rise in house prices after the contract; the seller
knew that the purchasers "had no financial resources beyond [the price] that they
could have put together for the purchase of [the seller's house] . . . [The pur-
chasers] were therefore to the [seller's] knowledge unable at the time of breach
to raise a further £1500 to purchase an equivalent house forthwith, and so . . .
mitigate their loss".536c

536a [1974] Ch. 30 (mentioned in para.26–096, n.527).
536b On the relevance of this knowledge, see this Supplement, para.26–095B, above.
536c [1974] Ch. 30, 57.

Recovery of sum due on performance

[*Add to note 572: page* [1487]]   **26–107**
The *White and Carter* case was further distinguished where one party's
obligation to pay a definite sum was not dependent on performance by the other
party of its own obligations: *Ministry of Sound (Ireland) Ltd v World On-line Ltd*
[2003] EWHC 2178 (Ch); [2003] 2 All E.R. (Comm.) 823.

6. PENALTY OR LIQUIDATED DAMAGES

Statement of penalty rules

[*Add to note 599: page* [1490]]   **26–110**
The law laid down in the *Dunlop* case has not been significantly altered by the
Philips Hong Kong case (cited in para.26–109, n.589 above): *Jeancharm Ltd v
Barnet Football Club Ltd* [2003] EWCA Civ 58; [2003] 92 Con. L. R. 26.

[*Add to note 605: page* [1491]]
cf. *Jeancharm Ltd v Barnet Football Club Ltd*, above, n.599 (interest rate for
late payment of 5 per cent per week held to be a penalty).

8. INTEREST AND RATE OF EXCHANGE

Finance charges on particular transaction contemplated

[*Add to note 788: page* [1511]]   **26–145**
On the relevance of the impecuniosity of the claimant, see paras 26–095A—
26–095D, above.

CHAPTER 27

SPECIFIC PERFORMANCE AND INJUNCTION

2. THE "ADEQUACY" OF DAMAGES

Sale of goods: non-delivery

27–014   [*Add to note 52, line 6, after reference to Lingen v Simpson: page* [1528]]
   cf. Land Rover Group Ltd v UPF (UK) Ltd [2002] EWHC 3183; [2003] B.C.L.C. 222 at [52] (mandatory injunction to enforce obligation to supply chassis to car manufacturer).

Specific enforcement of contracts not within section 52

27–017   [*Add to note 70: page* [1530]]
   cf. Land Rover Group Ltd v UPF (UK) Ltd [2002] EWHC 3183; [2003] 2 B.C.L.C. 222, above para.27–014 of this Supplement. For the question whether the goods in that case were indeed specific (as was there agreed: see at [52]) *cf.* Main Work, para.43–031.

Thank you for purchasing **Chitty on Contracts**, 1st Supplement to the 29th edition.

Supplements to your main work

Chitty will be supplemented regularly in order to keep your main work up-to-date with ongoing developments.

In order to receive your updating supplements to **Chitty** automatically on publication you need to register. Supplements will be invoiced on publication. You can cancel your request at any time.

How to register

Either complete and return this FREEPOST card, or, if you have purchased your copy of **Chitty** from a bookshop or other supplier, please ask your supplier to ensure that you are registered to receive your supplements.

THOMSON™

SWEET & MAXWELL

Yes, please send me updating supplements to **Chitty on Contracts** on publication, unless countermanded.

Name

Organisation

Address

Postcode

Telephone

Email

S&M account number (if known)

Signed   Date

LEGAL BUSINESS UNIT

SWEET & MAXWELL LTD

FREEPOST LON 12091

LONDON

NW3 4YS

UNITED KINGDOM

7. Specific Performance With Compensation

Condition against error or misdescription

[Substitute for note 306: page [1554]]

The Court of Appeal has held that the Unfair Terms in Consumer Contracts Regulations 1999 (SI 1999/2083), apply to contracts for the sale of an interest in land by a commercial supplier to a consumer: *London Borough of Newham v Khatun* [2004] EWCA Civ 55; [2004] 3 W.L.R. 417, see above, para.15–014.

27–056

8. Injunction

Negative contracts

[Add to note 323: page [1556]]

For the application of the "balance of convenience" test to a mandatory injunction to enforce a position obligation (to maintain supplies of components to the supplier of motor vehicles), see *Land Rover Group Ltd v UPF (UK) Ltd* [2002] EWHC 3183; [2003] B.C.L.C. 222 at [60]. The injunction there granted was an interim injunction (at [65]), so that the "balance of convenience" test was applicable also on the principle stated in Main Work, para.27–060.

27–059

Statutory provisions against refusal to contract

[Add to note 386, line 3, after reference to SI 1996/438: page [1564]]

For the unlawfulness of discrimination on grounds of religion or belief, and for remedies in respect of such discrimination, see Employment Equality (Religion or Belief) Regulations 2003 (SI 2003/1660). Regulation 30 falls short of providing for injunctive relief: it enables an employment tribunal to make a "recommendation" that steps should be taken to obviate or reduce the adverse effect on the complainant of the discrimination (reg.30(1)(c)); but the only effect of failure to comply with the recommendation is to increase the compensation payable to the complainant or to enable him to get compensation where no order for compensation was originally made (reg.30(3)). The position is the same in cases of unlawful discrimination on grounds of sexual orientation: see Employment Equality (Sexual Orientation) Regulations 2003 (SI 2003/1661), reg.30.

27–072

CHAPTER 28

LIMITATION OF ACTIONS

1. PERIODS OF LIMITATION

Latent damage in actions for the tort of negligence

28–010   [*Add to note 47: page* [1575]]

It has also been held that the Limitation Act 1980, s.14A does not apply to a claim for damages under s.2(1) of the Misrepresentation Act 1967 because under s.2(1) there is no onus on the claimant to prove negligence: *Laws v The Society of Lloyd's* [2003] EWCA Civ 1887; *The Times*, January 23, 2004, at [78]–[93].

5. EXTENSION OF THE PERIOD

(b) *Fraud, Concealment or Mistake*

Concealment

28–086   [*Add to note 329: page* [1602]]

In *Williams v Fanshaw Porter & Hazelhurst* [2004] EWCA Civ 157; [2004] 2 All E.R. 616, the decision in *Cave v Robinson Jarvis & Rolf* [2002] UKHL 18;

[2003] 1 A.C. 384 was considered and applied to a professional negligence claim. It was held that a trainee legal executive, employed by the defendants, had deliberately concealed a relevant fact within the meaning of s.32(1)(b) of the Limitation Act 1980.

(d) *Agreement of the Parties*

Estoppel

[Add to note 427; page [1611]]   **28–109**
Super Chem Products Ltd v American Life and General Insurance Co Ltd [2004] UKPC 2; [2004] 2 All E.R. 358.

7. Commencement of Proceedings

Amendments to statement of case after the end of the limitation period

[Add to note 471: page [1615]]   **28–118**
Laws v The Society of Lloyd's [2003] EWCA Civ 1887; *The Times,* January 23, 2004.

Part Nine

RESTITUTION

CHAPTER 29

RESTITUTION

1. INTRODUCTION

(c) *The Theoretical Basis of Restitution*

Different causes of action within restitution

29–017   [*Add to note 79: page* [1642]]

See also *Criterion Properties Ltd v Stratford UK Properties* [2004] UKHL 28; [2004] 1 W.L.R. 1846, at [4] (Lord Nicholls).

2. Unjust Enrichment

(b) *Enrichment*

Service resulting in incontrovertible benefit

[Add to end of note 116: page [1645]]
See Virgo (2004) C.L.J. 280.

(e) *Mistake*

Burden of proof

[Add to note 174, after reference to Kleinwort Benson case: page [1652]]
Cobbold v Bakewell Management Ltd [2003] EWHC 2289 (Ch), at [19]
(Rimer J.).

Mistake of law: principles governing recovery

[Add to note 249: page [1661]]
In *Brennan v Bolt Burdon* [2004] EWCA Civ 1017 Maurice Kay L.J. stated
that he was "reluctant to countenance as a mistake of law a situation in which it
is generally known or ought to be known that the law in question is about to be
reconsidered on appeal."

[Add new note 249a after "compromise" in line 10: page [1661]]
249a See *Brennan v Bolt Burdon* [2004] EWCA Civ 1017.

Changes in the law.

[Add to note 261 in line 3, after reference to Derrick v Williams: page [1662]]
See also *Brennan v Bolt Burdon* [2004] EWCA Civ 1017, especially at [50]
(Bodey J.).

(g) *Ultra vires Receipts by the Revenue and Public Authorities*

Ultra vires demands.

[Add to note 452: page [1684]]
See further *Sempra Metals Ltd v Inland Revenue Commissioners* [2004]
EWHC 2387 (Ch).

(h) *Compulsion*

Compulsory payments to a third person

[Delete final sentence in note 539: page [1693], *and replace with:*]
See also *Niru Battery Manufacturing Co v Milestone Trading Ltd (No.2)*
[2004] EWCA Civ 487; [2004] 2 All E.R. (Comm.) 289 where the "principles of
recoupment" were applied, although the effect was to recognise a restitutionary
claim founded on the ground of legal compulsion.

The defendant must be primarily or ultimately liable to pay the third person

29–102   [*Add to the end of note 551: page* [1695]]
     See also *Niru Battery Manufacturing Co v Milestone Trading Ltd (No.2)* [2004] EWCA Civ 487; [2004] 2 All E.R. (Comm.) 289 where restitution was available even though the claimant and the defendant were not subject to a common demand.

The right to contribution.

29–121   [*Delete the final sentence in note 631: page* [1705] *and replace with:*]
     However, in *Niru Battery Manufacturing Co v Milestone Trading Ltd (No.2)* [2004] EWCA Civ 487; [2004] 2 All E.R. (Comm.) 289 the Court of Appeal suggested that, if it had been necessary to decide the point, the dicta in *Royal Brompton Hospital Trust* concerning the meaning of "damage" were *obiter* and that it was bound by the earlier decision of the Court of Appeal in *Friends' Provident Life Office v Hillier Parker May and Rowden (a firm)* [1997] Q.B. 85, which held that a claim for restitution could be treated as a claim for compensation for the purposes of the 1978 Act, so that claims for breach of contract or tort and for unjust enrichment could be treated as claims for the same damage.

(j) *Exploitation*

Undue influence

29–137   [*Add to note 698: page* [1712]]
     See *Yorkshire Bank plc v Tinsley* [2004] EWCA Civ 816; [2004] 3 All E.R. 463.

3. Restitution for Wrongs

(b) *Tort*

Which torts may give rise to a restitutionary claim

29–142   [*Add to note 732: page* [1715]]
     In *Severn Trent Water Ltd v Barnes* [2004] EWCA Civ 570 damages for trespass to land were awarded to compensate the claimant for the loss of opportunity to bargain with the defendant for the price of interfering with the claimant's land rather than to deprive the defendant of any gain made by committing the tort.

The nature of the benefit

29–144   [*Add to note 751, line 6 after reference to Wrotham Park Estate case: page* [1717]]
     Severn Trent Water Ltd v Barnes [2004] EWCA Civ 570.

(c) *Breach of Contract*

Restitution for breach of contract

[*Add to note 796, at end: page* [1721]]   **29–151**
Amec Developments v Jury's Hotel Management [2001] E.G.L.R. 81. See also
O'Brien Homes Ltd v Lane [2004] EWHC 303 (QB) where damages for breach
of a collateral contract not to build more than three houses were assessed by
reference to what the defendant would have been prepared to pay the claimant to
be released from the contractual obligation.

(d) *Equitable Wrongdoing*

Types of equitable wrongdoing

[*Add to note 809: page* [1723]]   **29–155**
Crown Dilmun, Dilmun Investments Ltd v Nicholas Sutton, Fulham River
[2004] EWHC 52 (Ch); *Re Quarter Master UK Ltd* (Paul Morgan Q.C.) (July 15,
2004).

Receipt of a bribe, secret profit or commission

[*Text to note 817: page* [1724]]   **29–156**
In *Daraydan Holdings Ltd v Solland* [2004] EWHC 622 (Ch) Lawrence
Collins J. recognised that a defendant who had received a secret commission
from the claimants in breach of fiduciary duty held that commission on con-
structive trust for the claimants, following the decision of the Privy Council in
Attorney General for Hong Kong v Reid [1994] 1 A.C. 324.

Equitable allowance

[*Add to note 823: page* [1725]]   **29–157**
The award of an equitable allowance was declined in *Re Quarter Master UK
Ltd* (July 15, 2004) on the ground that directors should not profit from their
breach of fiduciary duty and that the directors concerned had not demonstrated
special skills or taken unusual risks.

4. PROPRIETARY RESTITUTIONARY CLAIMS

(a) *Establishing proprietary rights*

Constructive trusts

[*Add to note 837, in line 10, after reference to Att.-Gen. (HK) v Reid: page* [1726]]   **29–160**
: approved in *Daraydan Holdings Ltd v Solland International Ltd* [2004]
EWHC 622 (Ch) (Lawrence Collins J.).

[Add to note 843: page [1727]]
   Cobbold v Bakewell Management Ltd [2003] EWHC 2289 (Ch), at [17] (Rimer J.).

(c) *Proprietary restitutionary claims*

Subrogation

29–173
   [Add to note 919: page [1734]]
   Cheltenham and Gloucester plc v Appleyard [2004] EWCA Civ 291.

[Add to note 920, after reference to Eagle Star Insurance v Karasiewicz]
   Filby v Mortgage Express (No.2) Ltd [2004] EWCA Civ 759 (where, although the claim was characterised as grounded on unjust enrichment, the court treated it as a claim founded on the vindication of property rights).

[Add to note 919]
   See also *Niru Battery Manufacturing Co v Milestone Trading Ltd (No.2)* [2004] EWCA Civ 487; [2004] 2 All E.R. (Comm.) 289, where the remedy of subrogation was ordered to prevent the defendant's unjust enrichment arising from the discharge of a liability owed by the defendant. It is unclear, however, why this remedy was sought or obtained since the claimant had a direct restitutionary claim to recover the value of the benefit obtained by the defendant and did not need to step into the shoes of any other party to bring such a claim.

[In note 925, replace reference to Niru Battery Manufacturing Co v Milestone Trading Ltd (No.2): page [1735] with]
   [2004] EWCA Civ 487; [2004] 2 All E.R. (Comm.) 289.

[Add to note 927]
   See also *Cheltenham and Gloucester plc v Appleyard* [2004] EWCA Civ 291, at [32] (Neuberger L.J.).

[Add to the end of note 930]
   See also *Filby v Mortgage Express (No.2)* [2004] EWCA Civ 758, where a mortgage was a nullity by virtue of a forged signature; and *Cheltenham and Gloucester plc v Appleyard* [2004] EWCA Civ 291, where a mortgage had not been registered.

[Add to the end of note 932]
   Compare *Cheltenham and Gloucester plc v Appleyard* [2004] EWCA Civ 291, where the claimant's mortgage had not been registered as required by statute but it was subrogated to another mortgage because, *inter alia*, the claimant had not obtained the legal charge for which it had bargained but only an equitable charge and the failure to register was not the result of the claimant's negligence.

[Add to note 935, after reference to Banque Financière de la Cité case: page [1736]]
   Cheltenham and Gloucester plc v Appleyard [2004] EWCA Civ 291, at [36] (Neuberger L.J.).

[Add to the text at the end of the paragraph]

Principles relating to the award of the equitable remedy of subrogation were usefully summarised by the Court of Appeal in *Cheltenham and Gloucester plc v Appleyard*.[936a] These include that a lender cannot claim subrogation if he obtains all of the security for which he bargained[936b] or where the lender bargained on the basis that no security would be received.[936c]

[936a] [2004] EWCA Civ 291, at [32]–[44] (Neuberger L.J.).
[936b] *Capital Finance Co Ltd v* Stokes [1969] 1 Ch. 261.
[936c] *Paul v Speirway Ltd (in liquidation)* [1976] 1 W.L.R. 220.

Personal restitutionary remedies

[Add to note 937, at the end: page [1736]]   **29–174**

The House of Lords concluded that the case was not concerned with the question of unconscionability but whether directors had authority to sign an agreement: [2004] UKHL 28; [2004] 1 W.L.R. 1846. On the interpretation of the test of unconscionability see also *Crown Dilmun, Dilmun Investments Ltd v Nicholas Sutton, Fulham River* [2004] EWHC 52 (Ch), at [200] (Peter Smith J.).

5. DEFENCES

(b) *Change of position*

Change of position as a separate defence

[Add to note 972: page [1740]]   **29–179**

Barros Mattos Jnr v McDaniels Ltd [2004] EWHC 1188 (Ch); [2004] 3 All E.R. 299, at [16] (Laddie J.).

[Add to the text after note 973 in line 4]

In *Commerzbank AG v Gareth Price-Jones*[973a] Mummery L.J. recognised that "the decided cases steer a cautious course, aiming to avoid the dangers of a diffuse discretion and the restrictions of rigid rules." Munby J. stated that the defence was "intended to be a broadly stated concept of practical justice" and that "technicality and black letter law are to be avoided."[973b]

[973a] [2003] EWCA Civ 1663; [2004] 1 P. & C.R. D. 15, at [32].
[973b] *Ibid.*, at [48]

Illustrations of change of position

[Add to note 984: page [1741]]   **29–180**

The Court of Appeal expressly recognised that an anticipatory change of position is a good defence in *Commerzbank AG v Gareth Price-Jones* [2003] EWCA Civ 1663; [2004] 1 P. & C.R. D. 15, at [38] (Mummery L.J.) and [64] (Munby J.).

Link between receipt and specific expenditure unnecessary

29–181   [*Add to end of paragraph: page* [1742]]
In *Commerzbank AG v Gareth Price-Jones*[992a] the Court of Appeal recognised that a non-pecuniary change of position may be sufficient to establish the defence, although, on the facts of the case, the defendant's change of position in staying in his job rather than seeking more lucrative employment elsewhere was not sufficient for it to be inequitable to require him to make restitution since there was no relevant connection between the anticipated receipt of money and the decision to stay in his job and that decision did not have a significant, precise or substantial impact on the defendant.

[992a] [2003] EWCA Civ 1663; [2004] 1 P. & C.R. D. 15, at [39], [40], [43] (Mummery L.J.) and [59] (Munby J.).

Bad faith

29–183   [*Add to footnote 1002a: page* [1743]]
See also *Commerzbank AG v Gareth Price-Jones* [2003] EWCA Civ 1663; [2004] 1 P & C.R. D. 15, para.[53] where Munby J. stated that this was an exercise in judicial evaluation rather than judicial discretion. Cp. Birks (2004) 120 LQR 373, Burrows (2004) C.L.J. 276.

[*Add to text at end of paragraph*]
The defence is not available where a defendant's change of position is tainted since it involves the commission of an illegal act, other than where the illegality can be characterised as *de minimis*.[1004a]

[1004a] *Barros Mattos Jnr v McDaniels Ltd* [2004] EWHC 1188 (Ch); [2004] 3 All E.R. 299.

Relative fault

29–184   [*Add to text at end of paragraph: page* [1744]]
However, in *Commerzbank AG v Gareth Price-Jones*[1011a] Munby J., whilst acknowledging that relative fault was irrelevant, was clearly influenced by the fact that the defendant changed his position as a result of his own negligent mistake, which was not shared or induced by the claimant, in reaching his conclusion that it was not equitable to allow the defendant to rely on the defence.

[1011a] [2003] EWCA Civ 1663; [2004] 1 P & C.R. D. 15. See also *Niru Battery Manufacturing Co v Milestone Trading Ltd (No.2)* [2004] EWCA Civ 487, at [33] (Clarke L.J.).

(c) *Settlement of an honest claim*

Payer has doubts but nevertheless pays

29–187   [*Add to note 1020: page* [1746]]
Cobbold v Bakewell Management Ltd [2003] EWHC 2289 (Ch) at [19] (Rimer J.); *Brennan v Bolt Burdon* [2004] EWCA Civ 1017.

Compromise

[Add to text at end of paragraph: page [1747]]*

A compromise may be invalidated by a mistake, but not where the compromise was agreed on the basis of an erroneous assumption about the law.[1030a]

[1030a] *Brennan v Bolt Burdon* [2004] EWCA Civ 1017.

Part Ten

CONFLICT OF LAWS

CHAPTER 30

CONFLICT OF LAWS

1. PRELIMINARY CONSIDERATIONS

Sources of the law

30–002   *[Add in line 2 of note 4: page* [1758]*]*
King v Brandywine Reinsurance Co (UK) Ltd [2004] EWHC 1033 (Comm).

2. THE DOCTRINE OF THE PROPER LAW OF A CONTRACT

Incorporation by reference

30–008   *[Add at end of note 38: page* [1763]*]*
Shamil Bank of Bahrain v Beximco Pharmaceuticals Ltd [2004] EWCA Civ 19; [2004] 1 W.L.R. 1784 (a case on the Rome Convention).

3. THE ROME CONVENTION

(a) *In General*

[*Add to note 94: page* [1769]]
Meeusen, Pertegas and Straetmans (eds.), *Enforcement of International Contracts in the European Union* (2004).

History and purpose

[*Text at notes 100 and 101: page* [1769]]   **30–016**
Belgium finally ratified the Brussels Protocol on May 5, 2004. The Protocol entered into force on August 1, 2004.

Revision of the Rome Convention

[*Add to note 108: page* [1770]]   **30–018**
Meeusen, Pertegas and Straetmans (eds.), *Enforcement of International Contracts in the European Union* (2004).

[*Add at beginning of note 113: page* [1771]]
See the Opinion of the European Economic and Social Committee on the Green Paper at [2004] OJ C108/1.

[*Note 114: page* [1771]]
On the proposed "Rome II", see House of Lords, European Union Committee, *The Rome II Regulation: Report with Evidence*, HL Paper 66 (2004).

Interpretation: European Court of Justice

[*Text at notes 117 and 118: page* [1771]]   **30–019**
As a result of Belgian ratification of the Protocols on May 5, 2004, the Protocols entered into force on August 1, 2004.

Uniformity of interpretation and application

[*Add to note 131: page* [1773]]   **30–020**
Base Metal Trading v Shamurin [2003] EWHC 2419 (Comm); [2004] 1 All E.R. (Comm.) 159; *European Bank of Reconstruction & Development v Tekoglu* [2004] EWHC 846 (Comm); *Apple Corps Ltd v Apple Computer Inc* [2004] EWHC 768 (Ch).

Incorporation by reference

[*Add at beginning of note 154: page* [1776]]   **30–029**
Shamil Bank of Bahrain v Beximco Pharmaceuticals Ltd [2004] EWCA Civ 19; [2004] 1 W.L.R. 1784.

[*Note 154: page* [1776]]

The principle of incorporation by reference only applies where the parties have sufficiently indicated the provisions of a foreign law or international convention which are apt to be incorporated as terms of the contract. A broad reference to principles of Sharia law is insufficient to incorporate such principles: *Shamil Bank of Bahrain v Beximco Pharmaceuticals Ltd*, above.

(b) *Exclusions*

Meaning of "contractual obligations"

30–031   [*Add at end of note 159: page* [1777]]

Pertegas in Meeusen, Pertegas and Straetmans (eds.) *Enforcement of International Contracts in the European Union* (2004), pp.175–190; Briggs [2003] L.M.C.L.Q. 12.

[*Add at end of note 160: page* [1778]]
As to unilateral contracts, see Maher, 2002 Jur. Rev. 317.

Concurrent liability

30–032   [*Add in first line of note 163: page* [1778]]
    cf. Base Metal Trading Ltd v Shamurin [2003] EWHC 2419 (Comm); [2004] 1 All E.R. (Comm.) 159.

Restitution

30–033   [*Add at end of note 170: page* [1779]]
    cf. Caterpillar Financial Services Corporation v SNC Passion [2004] EWHC 569 (Comm.), at [16].

Wills, succession, etc.

30–036   [*Add to note 175: page* [1779]]
Bogdan in Meeusen, Pertegas and Straetmans (eds.), *The Enforcement of International Contracts in the European Union* (2004), pp.211–223.

Arbitration agreements and agreements on the choice of court

30–039   [*Add to note 190; page* [1780]]
Morse in Meeusen, Pertegas and Straetmans (eds.), *The Enforcement of International Contracts in the European Union* (2004), pp.191–209.

Questions governed by the law of companies, etc.

30–040   [*Add to note 202: page* [1781]]
Benedetelli in Meeusen, Pertegas and Straetmans (eds.), *The Enforcement of International Contracts in the European Union* (2004), pp.225–254.

Insurance

[*Note 224: page* [1784]]   **30–044**
Update reference to *Dicey & Morris* to *Dicey & Morris op. cit. Fourth
Supplement to the 13th ed.* (2004), r.184, pp.398–411.

[*Note 228: page* [1784]]
Update reference to *Dicey & Morris* to *Dicey & Morris op. cit. Fourth
Supplement to the 13th ed.* (2004), r.185, pp.412–426, r.186, pp.427–435.

Identification of *situs*

[*Note 232: page* [1785]]   **30–045**
Update reference to *Dicey & Morris* to *Dicey & Morris op. cit. Fourth
Supplement to the 13th ed.* (2004), pp.403–405.

(c) *Choice of Law by the Parties*

Choice must be of law of a country

[*Add to note 236: page* [1786]]   **30–047**
Shamil Bank of Bahrain v Beximco Pharmaceuticals Ltd [2004] EWCA Civ
19; [2004] 1 W.L.R. 1784.

[*Add to note 237: page* [1786]]
Shamil Bank of Bahrain v Beximco Pharmaceuticals Ltd, above (choice of
principles of Sharia law not a choice of the law of a country).

"Implied choice"

[*Add to note 253: page* [1787]]   **30–050**
*Travelers Casualty & Surety Co of Europe v Sun Life Insurance Co of Canada
(UK) Ltd* [2004] EWHC 1704 (Comm).

[*Add in line 5 of note 256: page* [1787]]
Evialis S.A. v S.I.A.T. [2003] EWHC 863 (Comm); [2003] 2 Lloyd's Rep. 377;
Tonicstar Ltd v American Home Insurance Co [2004] EWHC 1234 (Comm).

[*Add in line 7 of note 260: page* [1788]]
European Bank of Reconstruction & Development v Tekoglu [2004] EWHC
846 (Comm).

[*Add at end of note 262: page* [1788]]
See also Morse in Meeusen, Pertegas and Straetmans (eds.), *The Enforcement
of International Contracts in the European Union* (2004), pp.191, 204–206.

Partial choice of law

30–054 *[Add in line 7 of note 283: page* [1790]]
Travelers Casualty & Surety Co v Sun Life Assurance Co of Canada (UK) Ltd
[2004] EWHC 1704 (Comm).

Mandatory rules

30–059 *[Add to note 307: page* [1793]]
For a case where the application of Art.3(3) of the Rome Convention was
considered but rejected, see *Caterpillar Financial Services Corporation v SNC
Passion* [2004] EWHC 569 (Comm).

Public policy

30–067 *[Add to note 340: page* [1798]]
See also *Re COLT Telecom Group plc* [2002] EWHC 2815 (Ch); [2003]
B.P.I.R. 324; *Tekron Resources Ltd v Guinea Investment Co Ltd* [2003] EWHC
2577 (Comm); [2004] 2 Lloyd's Rep. 26.

"Community public policy"

30–068 *[Add to note 341: page* [1798]]
Peruzzetto in Meeusen, Pertegas and Straetmans (eds.), *The Enforcement of
International Contracts in the European Union* (2004), pp.343–361.

(d) *Applicable Law in the Absence of Choice by the Parties*

[Add in line 4 of note 346: page [1799]]
Hill (2004) 53 I.C.L.Q. 325; Atrill (2004) 53 I.C.L.Q. 549.

General principle

30–069 *[Add in last line of note 351: page* [1799]]
*Travelers Casualty & Surety Co of Europe Ltd v Sun Life Assurance Co of
Canada (UK) Ltd* [2004] EWHC 1704 (Comm).

Characteristic performance

30–072 *[Add to note 358: page* [1801]]
Hill (2004) 53 I.C.L.Q. 325; Atrill (2004) 53 I.C.L.Q. 549.

Characteristic performance not determinable

30–074 *[Add to note 367: page* [1802]]
Apple Corps Ltd v Apple Computer Inc [2004] EWHC 768 (Ch) (characteristic
performance of an agreement between two companies regulating the use of their
respective trade marks cannot be determined).

Specific applications

[*Add in line 5 of note 386: page* [1803]]   **30–075**
Marconi Communications International Ltd v PT Pan Indonesia Bank Ltd Tbk
[2004] EWHC 129 (Comm); [2004] 1 Lloyd's Rep. 594.

Characteristic performance cannot be determined

[*Add to notes 436 and 437: page* [1810]]   **30–087**
Apple Corps Ltd v Apple Computer Inc [2004] EWHC 768 (Ch).

Rebutting the presumptions

[*Add to note 438: page* [1810]]   **30–088**
Hill (2004) 53 I.C.L.Q. 325; Atrill (2004) 53 I.C.L.Q. 549.

[*Add to note 456: page* [1812]]
*cf. Marconi Communications International Ltd v PT Pan Indonesia Bank Ltd
Tbk* [2004] EWHC 129 (Comm); [2004] 1 Lloyd's Rep. 594 (letter of credit
issued by Indonesian bank which became insolvent, confirmed by another Indonesian bank with no place of business in England, the credit to be advised
through an English bank which did not confirm credit, documents to be presented
in England and payment to be made there, led to conclusion that although
presumptively the contract between the beneficiary and the confirming bank was
governed by Indonesian law, pursuant to Art.4(2) of the Rome Convention, the
above connections with England justified disregarding the presumption, pursuant
to Art.4(5)).

[*Add to note 459: page* [1812]]
See also *Marconi Communications International Ltd v PT Pan Indonesia Bank
Ltd Tbk*, above.

(e) *Certain Consumer Contracts and Individual Employment Contracts*

"Certain consumer contracts"

[*Add in line 5 of note 462: page* [1812]]   **30–090**
Basedow in Meeusen, Pertegas and Straetmans (eds.), *The Enforcement of
International Contracts in the European Union* (2004), pp.269–288; Straetmans
ibid. pp.295–322.

Individual employment contracts

[*Add in line 4 of note 526: page* [1822]]   **30–105**
Polak in Meeusen, Pertegas and Straetmans (eds.), *The Enforcement of International Contracts in the European Union* (2004), pp.323–342.

"Employment": autonomous meaning

30–107   [*Note 538: page* [1823]]
Base Metal Trading Ltd v Shamurin [2003] EWHC 2419 (Comm) is now reported at [2004] 1 All E.R. (Comm.) 159.

Choice of law by the parties and mandatory rules

30–109   [*Note 541: page* [1824]]
See previous entry.

[*Note 548: page* [1825]]
Serco Ltd v Lawson is now reported at [2004] I.C.R. 204.

[*Note 549: page* [1825]]
Race Relations Act 1976 is amended by Race Relations Act 1976 (Amendment) Regulations 2003 (SI 2003/1626), reg.11, inserting a new s.8(1A) into the principal Act. Disability Discrimination Act 1995 is amended by Disability Discrimination Act 1995 (Amendment) Regulations 2003 (SI 2003/1673), inserting a new s.68(1) and (2)–(4A) into the principal Act.

[*Add in line 4 of note 549: page* [1825]]
Employment Equality (Religion or Belief) Regulations 2003 (SI 2003/1660), reg.9; Employment Equality (Sexual Orientation) Regulations 2003 (SI 2003/1661), reg.9.

Applicable law in absence of choice

30–112   [*Add at beginning of note 559: page* [1826]]
See *Booth v Phillips* [2004] EWHC 1437 (Comm); *The Times*, July 27, 2004.

[*Add to note 560: page* [1826]]
Booth v Phillips, above.

30–113   [*Add to note 561: page* [1827]]
cf. Booth v Phillips, above.

[*Note 563: page* [1827]]
Base Metal Trading Ltd v Shamurin [2003] EWHC 2419 (Comm) is now reported at [2004] 1 All E.R. (Comm.) 159.

Contract and tort

30–114   [*Note 563: page* [1827]]
See previous entry.

[*Add in line 4 of note 564: page* [1827]]
Booth v Phillips [2004] EWHC 1437 (Comm).

(f) *Voluntary Assignments and Subrogation*

Voluntary assignments

[*Add at the end of note 570: page* [1828]]   **30–115**
Kieninger in Meeusen, Pertegas and Stratmans (eds.), *The Enforcement of International Contracts in the European Union* (2004), pp.363–387.

4. SCOPE OF THE APPLICABLE LAW

(d) *Particular Issues: Article 10*

Reservation of consequences of nullity

[*Add in line 7 of note 697: page* [1841]]   **30–141**
cf. Caterpillar Financial Services Corporation v SNC Passion [2004] EWHC 569 (Comm) at [16].

(e) *Illegality and Public Policy*

[*Add in line 5 of note 813: page* [1855]]
Peruzzetto in Meeusen, Pertegas and Straetmans (eds.), *The Enforcement of International Contracts in the European Union* (2004), pp.343–361.

[*Add at the end of note 813: page* [1855]]
Tekron Resources Ltd v Guinea Investment Co Ltd [2004] EWHC 2577 (Comm); [2004] 2 Lloyd's Rep. 26.

Act illegal under law of country where to be performed

[*Add in line 6 of note 823: page* [1587]]   **30–171**
Tekron Resources Ltd v Guinea Investment Co Ltd, above.

[*Add at end of note 828: page* [1857]]
Tekron Resources Ltd v Guinea Investment Co Ltd, above.

Public policy

[*Add to start of note 841: page* [1858]]   **30–173**
Re COLT Telecom Group plc [2002] EWHC 2815 (Ch); [2003] B.P.I.R. 324.

[*Add to note 850: page* [1860]]   **30–174**
See also *Tekron Resources Ltd v Guinea Investment Co Ltd* [2003] EWHC 2577 (Comm); [2004] 2 Lloyd's Rep. 26.

VOLUME II

SPECIFIC CONTRACTS

CHAPTER 31

AGENCY

1. AGENCY IN GENERAL

General and special agents

[*Add to note 64: page* [8]]   **31–011**
See on this general topic Brown [2004] J.B.L. 391.

3. CREATION OF AGENCY

(c) *Ratification*

Limits on ratification

[*Add to note 189: page* [20]]   **31–032**
See a further useful discussion by Keith J. (in the context of an originating
application issued without authority and ratified after expiry of a three month
time limit) in *Nottinghamshire Healthcare Trust v Prisons Officers Assn* [2003]
I.C.R. 1192, E.A.T.

(e) *Capacity*

Acting for both parties

[*Add to note 228: page* [24]]   **31–038**
But the point can arise in the context of conflict of interest also: see *Marks &
Spencer plc v Freshfields Bruckhaus Deringer* [2004] EWCA Civ 741.

(f) *Delegation*

Effect of delegation

[*Add to note 236: page* [25]]   **31–040**
See also *Heath Lambert Ltd v Sociedad de Corretaje de Seguros* [2003]
EWHC 2269 (Comm); [2004] 1 Lloyd's Rep. 495.

4. AUTHORITY

(a) *General Principles*

Express and implied authority

[*Add to note 258: page* [27]]   **31–042**
On the agent's lack of authority to act contrary to the principal's interest see
also *Hopkins v T.L.Dallas Group Ltd* [2004] EWHC 1379 (Ch); *Criterion
Properties plc v Stratford UK Properties LLC* [2004] UKHL 28; [2004] 1 W.L.R.
1846.

Implied authority: incidental authority

31–044   [*Add to note 263: page* [28]]
The word "necessarily" is not to be overstressed in this context: implied authority depends on consent, not on the rules for the implication of terms into contracts: *Targe Towing Ltd v Marine Blast Ltd* [2004] EWCA Civ 346; [2004] 1 Lloyd's Rep. 721 at [22].

5. PRINCIPAL'S RELATIONS WITH THIRD PARTIES

(b) *Apparent authority*

Apparent authority

31–056   [*Add to note 319: page* [34]]
In *Pacific Carriers Ltd v BNP Paribas* [2004] HCA 35 the High Court of Australia held a bank liable on a letter of indemnity against delivery without bill of lading which it had signed together with the shipper, its customer. The document had been stamped and signed by the Manager of the Documentary Credit Department of its Sydney office. The Manager intended to authenticate the signature of the shipper but on an objective interpretation of the document it was held that the signature was to an indemnity. The Manager had authority to sign authentications of signature but not promises of indemnity. There was no reason for the third party to know this and to the third party there was just a stamp accompanied by an illegible signature without description of the signer. The bank was held liable: its organisational structure and absence of procedures for such signatures meant that it had placed the signer in a position which equipped her to deal with letters of indemnity, and on this the third party had relied.

(c) *Undisclosed principal*

Undisclosed principal

31–061   [*Add to note 356: page* [38]]
See in general Tan Cheng-Han (2004) 120 L.Q.R. 480.

Meaning of "undisclosed principal"

31–063   [*Add to note 374: page* [40]]
The dangers of finding agency between related corporate structures are stressed by Langley J. in *Peterson Farms Inc v C & M Farming Ltd* [2004] EWHC 121 (Comm); [2004] 1 Lloyd's Rep. 603 at [62]; but *cf.* the *Rolls Royce* case, above.

[*Add to note 373: page* [40]]
Both the above cases were applied in *Rolls Royce Power Engineering plc v Ricardo Consulting Engineers Ltd* [2004] EWHC 2871; [2004] 2 All E.R. (Comm.) 129.

Exclusion of undisclosed principals

[*Add to note 392: page* [42]]   **31–065**
The *Siu Yin Kwan* case was applied in *Rolls Royce Power Engineering plc v Ricardo Consulting Engineers Ltd* [2004] EWHC 2871; [2004] 2 All E.R. (Comm.) 129, where it was held that the third party did not intend to deal with anyone on whose behalf the other party might be acting, and hence Rolls Royce as undisclosed principal could not intervene.

(d) *Further rules*

Agent acting in fraud of principal

[*Add to note 398: page* [42]]   **31–066**
See also *Criterion Properties plc v Stratford UK Properties LLC* [2004] UKHL 28; [2004] 1 W.L.R. 1846.

6. AGENT'S RELATIONS WITH THIRD PARTIES

(c) *Breach of Warranty of Authority*

Representation must be of fact and relied on

[*Add to note 611: page* [63]]   **31–101**
Enterprise Plus Ltd v Wagenmann [2003] EWHC 1827 (Comm).

7. OBLIGATIONS OF PRINCIPAL AND AGENT *INTER SE*

(a) *Duties of Agents*

(iii) *Loyalty*

Duty not to have conflicting interest

[*Add to note 717: page* [72]]   **31–120**
See also *Marks & Spencer Plc v Freshfields Bruckaus Deringer* [2004] EWCA Civ 741, holding that the conflicting interests can arise from different transactions with the same party.

(iv) *Remedies*

Equity: duty to account and equitable compensation

31–126   *[Add to note 752: page* [76]]
Att.-Gen for Hong Kong v Reid (a Privy Council case) was followed on this point by Lawrence Collins J. in *Daraydan Holdings Ltd v Solland International Ltd* [2004] EWHC 622 (Ch).

(b) *Rights of Agents*

(i) *Remuneration*

Right to remuneration

31–132   *[Insert new note 774a after "the principal" in line 1: page* [79]]
[774a] The agent's commission may sometimes be provided by the contract which he makes between principal and third party as payable to him. This is often held to create a trust in his favour: see *Les Affreteurs Reunis SA v Leopold Walford (London) Ltd* [1919] A.C. 801; see Main Work, Vol.1, paras 18–074 *et seq.* The agent may now be able to sue directly under the Contracts (Rights of Third Parties) Act 1999: see *ibid.*, paras 18–084 *et seq.* It has been held by Colman J. in such a context that an arbitration clause in the main contract applied to a claim by the agent as third party: *Nisshin Shipping Co Ltd v Cleaves & Co Ltd* [2003] EWHC 2602; [2004] 1 Lloyd's Rep. 38.

Where Commercial Agents Regulations applicable

31–147   *[Add to note 873: page* [90]]
In *Cooper v Pure Fishing (UK) Ltd* [2004] EWCA Civ 375 it was held that a principal who had cause for terminating the agency but chose not to renew it at its time of expiry had not "terminated" the contract for the purposes of the Regulations.

CHAPTER 32

ARBITRATION

1. STATUTORY REGULATION

Human Rights Act 1998

[*Add at end of note 49: page* [109]]   **32–016**
   Ghaidan v Godin-Mendoza [2004] UKHL 30; [2004] 3 W.L.R. 113 at
[37]–[52] (Lord Steyn).

2. THE ARBITRATION AGREEMENT

Scope of arbitration agreement

   The words "in relation to" a contract include disputes which are related to or   **32–025**
connected with it and cover a dispute concerning an alleged variation of the
contract: *El Nasharty v J Sainsbury plc* [2003] EWHC 2195 (Comm); [2004] 1
Lloyd's Rep. 308.

   [*Add in penultimate line of note 102, after reference to Capital Thrush Investments
   Ltd v Radio Design TJAB: page* [115]]
   Asghar v Legal Services Commission, The Times, August 5, 2004.

[91]

3. Stay of Legal Proceedings

Foreign proceedings

32–042   [*Add to note 150 in line 10, after reference to The Epsilon Rosa (No. 2): page [120]*]
Through Transport Mutual Insurance Association (Eurasia) Ltd v New India Assurance Co Ltd [2003] EWHC 3158 (Comm); [2004] 1 Lloyd's Rep. 206; *Atlanska Plovibda v Consignaciones Asturianas SA* [2004] EWHC 1273 (Comm); [2004] 2 Lloyd's Rep. 109 at [25].

[*Add after reference to Toepfer International GmbH v Société Cargill France in note 150, line 3 on page [121]*]
Navigation Maritime Bulgare v Rustal Trading Ltd [2002] 1 Lloyd's Rep. 107; *Through Transport Mutual Insurance Association (Eurasia) Ltd v New India Assurance Co Ltd*, above.

Discretionary stay

32–048   [*Page [123]*]
The court also has jurisdiction under CPR, r.11, to direct alternative dispute resolution notwithstanding the unwillingness of one party, but it will not order a stay of proceedings pending the attendance at mediation of a named non-party: *Shirayama Shokusan Co Ltd v Danovo Ltd* [2003] EWHC (Ch); [2004] B.L.R. 207.

[*Add at end of note 176*]
Contrast *El Nasharty v J Sainsbury plc* [2003] EWHC 2195 (Comm); [2004] 1 Lloyd's Rep. 309 at [29] (court must be "virtually certain" that there is an arbitration agreement before it grants a stay).

Claims indisputably due

32–049   [*Delete note 178 and substitute: page [124]*]
Now CPR, Pt 24.

4. Commencement of Arbitral Proceedings

Power of the court to extend time for beginning arbitral proceedings

32–054   [*Add to note 203: page [127]*]
See also *Thompson Monella v Pizza Express (Restaurants) Ltd* [2003] EWHC 2966 (Ch); [2004] 12 E.G. 172 (change in the law not outside the reasonable contemplation of the parties and in any event did not contribute to the failure to observe the time-limit).

Commencement of arbitral proceedings

[*Page* [128]]   **32–059**
In *Atlanska Plovidba v Consignaciones Asturianas SA* [2004] EWHC 1273
(Comm); [2004] 2 Lloyd's Rep. 109 at [17] Moore-Bick J. said:

> "If a notice of arbitration is to be effective, it must identify the dispute to which it
> relates with sufficient particularity and must also make it clear that the person giving
> it is intending to refer the dispute to arbitration, not merely threatening to do so if his
> demands are not met. Apart from that, however, I see no need for any further
> requirements. Whether any particular document meets those requirements will
> depend on its terms which must be understood in the context in which it was written.
> The weight of authority supports a broad and flexible approach to this ques-
> tion . . ."

Appointment of arbitrators

[*Page* [129]]   **32–061**
See *Atlanska Plovidba v Consignaciones Asturianas SA* [2004] EWHC 1273
(Comm); [2004] 2 Lloyd's Rep. 109 at [17]; para.32–059, above.

Failure of appointment procedure

[*note 243: page* [131]]   **32–065**
The reference for *Durtnell (R) & Sons Ltd v Secretary of State for Trade and
Industry* should be [2001] 1 Lloyd's Rep. 275.

[*Add at end of note 243*]
See also *Atlanska Plovidba v Consignaciones Asturianas SA* [2004] EWHC
1273 (Comm); [2004] 2 Lloyd's Rep. 109 (existence of concurrent judicial
proceedings in Spain not a ground for refusing appointment).

7. THE ARBITRAL PROCEEDINGS

Power to appoint experts etc

[*Add to note 354: page* [142]]   **32–089**
See the Chartered Institute of Arbitrators' guidelines on the use of tribunal-
appointed experts, legal advisers and assessors: (2004) *Arbitration* 70(1),
45–50.

Provisional relief with agreement of parties

[*Add to note 369: page* [144]]   **32–093**
Rastner v Jason, unreported, March 23, 2004 (Lightman J.) (freezing
order).

8. POWERS OF THE COURT

Court powers in support of arbitral proceedings

32–100   [*Add to note 396: page* [146]]
But see *BNP Paribas v Deloitte and Touche LLP* [2003] EWHC 2874 (Comm); [2004] 1 Lloyd's Rep. 233 (no power to order disclosure from non-party).

32–101   [*Add to note 400: page* [147]]
Hiscox Underwriting Ltd v Dickson Manchester & Co Ltd [2004] EWHC 49; [2004] 1 All E.R. (Comm.) 753 (interim order for disclosure).

[*Add to note 402*]
Hiscox Underwriting Ltd v Dickson Manchester & Co Ltd, above (arbitrator newly appointed and unfamiliar with case and so, in effect, unable to act).

9. THE AWARD

Conflict of laws

32–109   [*Add to note 428: page* [149]]
See *Peterson Farms Inc v C&M Farming Ltd* [2004] EWHC 121 (Comm); [2004] 1 Lloyd's Rep. 603 at [46].

Remedies

32–111   [*Add at end of note 436: page* [150]]
a freezing order (*Kastner v Jason*, unreported, March 23, 2004 (Lightman J.))

Interest

32–112   [*Add to note 446: page* [151]]
See Altaras (2004) *Arbitration* 70(2), 108. *cf. Durham CC v Darlington BC* [2003] EWHC 2598; [2004] B.L.G.R. 311 (no power to award interest for the period before the principal sum became payable).

Award as a defence

32–123   [*Page* [154]]
The effect of an award as between a party and a stranger was considered by Toulson J. in *Lincoln National Life Insurance Co v Sun Life Assurance Co of Canada* [2004] EWHC 343 (Comm); [2004] 1 Lloyd's Rep. 737. The same rules apply to arbitration awards as to judgments (at [53]). But "it is probably only at the level of the House of Lords that the rules to which a judgment or award between A and B may be relied upon by or against B in proceedings between B

and C, when those proceedings involve an issue between A and B, could be comprehensively reconsidered" (at [92]).

11. Powers of the Court in relation to the Award

Challenging the award: substantive jurisdiction

[*Add to note 536: page* [158]]   **32–132**
  Zaporozhyve Production Society v Ashly Ltd [2002] EWHC 1410 (Comm); *Peoples Insurance Co of China v Vysanthi Shipping Co Ltd* [2003] EWHC 1655 (Comm); [2003] 2 Lloyd's Rep. 617; *Peterson Farms Inc v C&M Farming Ltd* [2004] EWHC 121 (Comm). [2004] 1 Lloyd's Rep. 603 at [18].

[*Add to note 540*]   **32–133**
  It may be appropriate in some cases for the court to grant an injunction under this sub-section to prevent the arbitration from going ahead rather than leaving it to the tribunal to decide: *Zaporozhyve Production Society v Ashly Ltd* [2002] EWHC 1410 (Comm).

Challenging the award: serious irregularity

[*Add to note 554: page* [1603]]   **32–136**
  Bulfracht (Cyprus) Ltd v Boneset Shipping Co Ltd [2002] EWHC 2292 (Comm); [2002] 2 Lloyd's Rep. 681.

Challenge or appeal: restrictions and time-limits

[*Add to note 607: page* [166]]   **32–149**
  cf., Peterson Farms Inc v C&M Farming Ltd [2004] EWHC 121 (Comm); [2004] 1 Lloyd's Rep. 603.

Challenge or appeal: supplementary orders

[*Add to note 609: page* [166]]   **32–150**
  cf., Peterson Farms Inc v C&M Farming Ltd [2003] EWHC 2298; [2004] 1 Lloyd's Rep. 614 (Tomlinson J.) (s.67 application).

Limitation

[*Add to end of note 664: page* [171]]   **32–164**
  Good Challenger Navegante SA v Metalexportimport SA [2003] EWCA Civ 1668; [2004] 1 Lloyd's Rep. 67 (acknowledgement).

12. Miscellaneous

Adjudication

32–169   *[Add to note 683: page* [173]]
Pegram Shopfitters Ltd v Tally Weijl (UK) Ltd [2003] EWCA Civ 1750 at
[8]

[Add to note 685]
But see *Pegram Shopfitters Ltd v Tally Weijl (UK) Ltd*, above (challenge to the
jurisdiction of the adjudicator).

CHAPTER 33

BAILMENT

2. POSSESSION AND RELATED MATTERS

Sub-bailment

[Add to note 122: page [189]*]* **33–026**

It is, however, necessary to distinguish between consent to a sub-bailment and consent to the creation of a direct contractual relationship between the bailor and the sub-bailee. The two are "conceptually different": see *Targe Towing Ltd v Marine Blast Ltd* [2004] EWCA Civ 346; [2004] 1 Lloyd's Rep. 721.

4. Bailments for Valuable Consideration

(b) Custody for Reward

(i) In General

Custody for reward

33–049   *[Add to note 255: page [202]]*
While it is not necessary as a matter of law for a bailee to show what the cause of the damage was, the identification of the cause may be a "significant pointer as to whether or not the bailee has exercised reasonable care": *Coopers Payne Ltd v Southampton Container Terminal Ltd* [2003] EWCA Civ 1223; [2004] 1 Lloyd's Rep. 331 at [29].

[Add to note 258 after reference to Levison case: page [203]]
Euro Cellular (Distribution) plc v Danzas Ltd t/a Danzas AEI Intercontinental [2003] EWHC 3161 (Comm); [2004] 1 Lloyd's Rep. 521 at [60]–[66].

CHAPTER 34

BILLS OF EXCHANGE AND BANKING

1. Negotiable Instruments

(b) *Bills of exchange*

(vii) *Discharge of bill*

Present scope of doctrine

34–136   [*Add new note 435a at the end of the first sentence: page* [319]]
    [435a] The defence of change of position is available against restitutionary claims based on unjust enrichment, but even then it is not open to a wrongdoer (*Lipkin Gorman (a firm) v Karpnale Ltd* [1991] 2 A.C. 548, 580). There is some doubt as to whether it is available against a restitutionary claim based on the vindication of property rights, where the action is subject to the bona fide purchaser for value defence (*Foskett v McKeown* [2001] 1 A.C. 102, 129; *Papamichael v National Westminster Bank* [2003] 1 Lloyd's Rep. 341, 376).

    [*Add to note 436 at the end*]
    Commerzbank AG v Gareth Price-Jones [2003] EWCA Civ 1663 (noted by Birks, (2004) 120 L.Q.R. 373).

Assessment

34–137   [*Delete note 438: page* [320] *and substitute*]
    Important recent cases on the availability of the change of position defence include: *Scottish Equitable plc v Derby* [2001] EWCA Civ 369; [2001] 2 All E.R. (Comm.) 274 and *Credit Suisse (Monaco) SA v Attar* [2004] EWHC 374 (Comm) (on the need for a causal link between the mistaken receipt and the change of position); *Dextra Bank & Trust Co Ltd v Bank of Jamaica* [2002] 1 All E.R. (Comm.) 193 and *Commerzbank AG v Gareth Price-Jones* [2003] EWCA Civ 1663 (on anticipatory change of position); *Niru Battery Manufacturing Co v Milestone Trading Ltd* [2002] EWHC 1425 (Comm); [2002] 2 All E.R. (Comm.) 705, 741, approved [2003] EWCA Civ 1446; [2004] 4 All E.R.

(Comm.) 193 (on what constitutes "bad faith"); *Barros Mattos Junior v MacDaniels Ltd* [2004] EWHC 1188 (Ch); [2004] 3 All E.R. 299 (on a change of position which constitutes an illegal action). See, generally, Vol. I, paras 29–179 *et seq.*

Tracing order

[*Add to note 440 at the end: page* [320]]   **34–138**
See also *Bank of America v Arnell* [1999] Lloyd's Rep. Bank. 399.

[*Add to note 441 at the end*]
Bishopsgate Investment Management Ltd v Homan [1995] Ch. 211, C.A.; *Box v Barclays Bank plc* [1998] Lloyd's Rep. Bank. 185, 203; *Shalson v Russo* [2003] EWHC 1637 (Ch) at [140]–[141]. See also Smith, [1995] C.L.J. 290.

(c) *Cheques*

(ii) *Crossed Cheques*

Negligence issue

[*Amend note 515: page* [332]]   **34–171**
Delete "*Linklaters v HKSB* [2003] 1 Lloyd's Rep. 545" and replace with "*Linklaters (a firm) v HSBC Bank plc* [2003] EWHC 1113 (Comm); [2003] 1 Lloyd's Rep. 545 (noted by Ellinger, (2004) 120 L.Q.R. 226)."

2. ASPECTS OF BANKING LAW

(a) *Bank regulation*

(i) *Overview*

Other legislative controls

[*Add new note 621a after "by October 9, 2004", 22 lines from the start of this*   **34–222**
paragraph: page [351]]
621a EC Directive 2002/65 was implemented in the United Kingdom through the Financial Services (Distance Marketing) Regulations 2004, (SI 2004/2095), which came into force on October 31, 2004.

[*Delete first two sentences of note 624 and substitute: page* [352]]   **34–224**
The Money Laundering Regulations 2003 (SI 2003/3075) came into force, for the most part, on March 1, 2004. These Regulations repeal and replace the Money Laundering Regulations 1993 (SI 1993/1933) as amended and the Money Laundering Regulations 2001 (SI 2001/3641).

(ii) *The regulation of deposit-taking*

Sanctions for unauthorised acceptance of deposits

34–236   [*Add to note 655 at end: page* [357]]
The court has jurisdiction under the Supreme Court Act 1981, s.37, to make an order freezing the bank accounts of third parties over which the person who has contravened the authorisation requirements of the 2000 Act has control. See *Financial Services Authority v Fitt* [2004] EWHC 1669 (Ch).

(b) *The Relationship of Banker and Customer*

(ii) *Definition of a customer*

Account in nominee's name

34–249   [*Delete the first sentence of note 693 and substitute: page* [363]]
Money Laundering Regulations 2003 (SI 2003/3075), which came into force, for the most part, on March 1, 2004, and which repeal and replace the Money Laundering Regulations 1993 (SI 1993/1933) as amended and the Money Laundering Regulations 2001 (SI 2001/3641) (see para.34–224 above).

(iv) *Fiduciary Relationship and Duty of Care*

Every day transactions

34–255   [*Add to note 708 at the end: page* [367]]
(noted by Ellinger, (2004) 120 L.Q.R. 226).

[*Add to note 711 at the end*]
Customs and Excise Comrs v Barclays Bank plc [2004] EWHC 122 (Comm); [2004] 2 All E.R. 789 (bank given notice of grant of freezing order over its customer's assets owes no duty to the third party who obtained the order to take reasonable care to prevent disposal of its customer's funds in breach of the order unless, prior to release of funds, the bank has by its conduct objectively assumed responsibility to that party to take such care).

(v) *Banks and Undue Influence*

Nature of the transaction

34–266   [*Add to note 743 at the end: page* [372]]
Mortgage Agency Services Number Two Ltd v Chater [2003] EWCA Civ 490; [2004] 1 P. & C.R. 4 (joint loan to mother and son).

Rescission

34–271   [*Add to note 762 at the end: page* [375]]
If the property subject to the security is jointly owned by a husband and wife then, even though the security may not be enforceable against the wife, it may be

against the husband, and so the court may still order the property to be sold, under the Trusts of Land and Appointment of Trustees Act 1996, s.14, in order to realise the husband's share: see *First National Bank plc v Achampong* [2003] EWCA Civ 487; [2004] 1 F.C.R. 18, noted by Thompson, [2003] Conv. 314.

[*Add to note 768 at the end: page* [376]]
Applied in *UCB Group Ltd v Hedworth* [2003] EWCA Civ 1717 (a case of sub-subrogation). By contrast, where an earlier charge is voidable for undue influence as against the husband and the bank, a replacement charge, taken out as a condition of discharging that earlier charge, will itself be voidable, even if undue influence was not operative at the time of such replacement: *Yorkshire Bank plc v Tinsley* [2004] EWCA Civ 816; [2004] 3 All E.R. 463 (see this Supplement, para.7–106A, above).

(vi) *Banks as Constructive Trustees*

Dishonest assistance

[*Add to note 795 at the end: page* [379]]   **34–279**
The nature of the accountability of the accessory or assister in equity, and the remedies available against him, are usefully examined by Elliott and Mitchell, (2004) 67 M.L.R. 16 (arguing that the assister is jointly and severally liable along with the trustee whom he has assisted).

Combined test of dishonesty

[*Add to note 815 at the end: page* [383]]   **34–288**
The Court of Appeal of New Zealand had also expressed (*obiter*) reservations about the subjective element of the combined test of dishonesty, see *US International Marketing Ltd v National Bank of New Zealand Ltd*, C.A. 144/02, October 28, 2003, at [62] and [78]–[79], noted by Yeo, (2004) 120 L.Q.R. 208.

(vii) *Duty of Secrecy*

Duty of Secrecy

[*Add to note 851 at end: page* [390]]   **34–304**
In general terms, a customer who opens an account at a bank in the UK must be taken to have accepted and be entitled to assume that the bank will act in accordance with applicable anti-money laundering and terrorism legislation (*Tayeb v HSBC Bank plc* [2004] EWHC 1529 (Comm) at [57], *per* Colman J.).

[*Add to note 852 at the end*]
See also *Rodaro v Royal Bank of Canada* (2002) 59 O.R. (3d) 74 (Ont. C.A.), noted by Ogilvie, (2004) 19 B.F.L.R. 103.

(c) *The Current Account*

(i) *Rights and Duties of the Banker*

Overdrafts

34–312   [*Add to note 878 at the end: page* [394]]
References to the bank's "usual rate of interest" or "usual terms" in standard form account opening agreements are not necessarily insufficiently certain to be enforceable as contract terms: whether such a provision fails for uncertainty depends on the evidence placed before the court: *Financial Institutions Services Ltd v Negril Negril Holdings Ltd* [2004] UKPC 40.

[*Add to note 880 at the end*]
affd. [2004] EWCA Civ 64 (but stating that the position would be otherwise where the bank had notice of the agreed limitation as between the account holders).

Effect of agreement

34–314   [*Add to note 891 at the end: page* [396]]
[2004] 2 Lloyd's Rep. 19, affd. [2004] EWCA Civ 1074.

Mandate and third parties

34–317   [*Add to note 907: page* [398]]
To similar effect, see *Tayeb v HSBC Bank plc* [2004] EWHC 1529 (Comm) at [75]–[77], *per* Colman J.

[*Add to note 908*]
In *Tayeb v HSBC Bank plc* [2004] EWHC 1529 (Comm), Colman J. held that mere suspicion as to the origin of funds transferred into a customer's bank account by a third party using the CHAPS electronic funds transfer system—as to which, see para.34–380 below—did not present the bank with a justifiable reason for returning those funds to the transferor without the customer's consent.

(ii) *Termination of Duty to Pay*

Third party debt orders

34–324   [*Add to note 933 at the end: page* [402]]
Kuwait Oil Tanker Co SAK v Qabazard is now reported at [2004] 1 A.C. 300 and is noted by Rogerson, [2003] C.L.J. 576; Briggs, [2003] L.M.C.L.Q. 418; Dickinson, (2004) 120 L.Q.R. 16.

(iii) *Protection of Paying Banker in Cases of Unauthorised Payment*

Pass book and periodic statement

[Add to note 957 in line 5, after reference to Royal Bank of Scotland plc v Fielding: **34–334**
page [406]]
affd. [2004] EWCA Civ 64.

[Add to note 960: page [407]]
See also *Financial Institutions Services Ltd v Negril Negril Holdings Ltd*
[2004] UKPC 40 (conclusive evidence clause was not clear and unambiguous
and so was construed narrowly against the bank).

(iv) *Special Types of Current Accounts*

Trust accounts

[Insert new note 1008a at the end of first sentence: page [415]] **34–350**
1008a For the nature of a trust account, see *Mann v Coutts & Co* [2003] EWHC 2138 (Comm);
[2004] 1 All E.R. (Comm.) 1 at [154]–[165].

(d) *Discount and Collection*

Non-transferable cheques

[Add to note 1021 at the end: page [417]] **34–353**
noted by Ellinger, (2004) 120 L.Q.R. 226.

Causes of action

[Add to note 1031 at the end: page [418]] **34–354**
noted by Ellinger, (2004) 120 L.Q.R. 226.

Instances of negligence

[Delete note 1042 and substitute: page [420]] **34–356**
1042 Money Laundering Regulations 2003 (SI 2003/3075) which came into force, for the most part,
on March 1, 2004. These new Regulations repeal and replace the Money Laundering Regulations
1993 (SI 1993/1933) as amended and the Money Laundering Regulations 2001 (SI 2001/3641) (see
para.34–224 above).

[Add to note 1047 at the end: page [421]] **34–357**
noted by Ellinger, (2004) 120 L.Q.R. 226.

(e) *The Giro System and Electronic Transfer of Funds*

Paper-based and electronic system

[Insert in the tenth line of the text after "BACS Ltd" and before "("BACS")": page **34–374**
[428]]
and, since December 1, 2003, BACS Payment Schemes Ltd,

Clearing house rules

34-379   [*Add to note 1096 at end: page [430]*]
See also *Tayeb v HSBC Bank plc* [2004] EWHC 1529 (Comm) at [57].

[*Amend note 1098*]
Update reference to New CHAPS Rules to Version 1.3, r.10.1.1.

UK clearing systems

34-380   [*Insert in the seventh line of the text after "BACS Ltd" and before "which provides": page [431]*]
and, since December 1, 2003, BACS Payment Schemes Ltd,

Cases where payee claims payment is complete

34-402   [*Add to text at end of paragraph: page [440]*]
Similarly, in *Tayeb v HSBC Bank plc*,[1137a] where the payee's bank became suspicious of the origin of funds transferred into the payee's account using the CHAPS electronic transfer system and returned those funds to the payer's bank, Colman J. held that a CHAPS transfer was ordinarily irreversible once the payee's bank had authenticated the transfer, sent an acknowledgement message informing the payer's bank that the transfer had been received and credited the funds to the payee's account.[1137b]

[1137a] [2004] EWHC 1529 (Comm).

[1137b] At [60] and [85]. However, the judge stated (at [60]) that there was an appropriate analogy with the practice in relation to documentary credits where, at the time of presentation of documents, a bank with cogent evidence of fraud can decline to make payment (*United Trading Corporation v Allied Arab Bank Ltd* [1985] 2 Lloyd's Rep. 554). He added (at [61]) that the same exception was likely to apply in respect of illegal transactions (see *Mahonia Ltd v JP Morgan Chase Bank* [2003] 2 Lloyd's Rep. 911).

Availability as if cash

34-406   [*Add to note 1142 at end: page [442]*]
See also *Tayeb v HSBC Bank plc* [2004] EWHC 1529 (Comm) at [88].

(i) *Bankers' Commercial Credits*

(iii) *The Contract between Seller and Buyer*

The documentary credit clause

34-470   [*Add to note 1241 at the end: page [467]*]
Provision of a letter of credit is a condition precedent to any obligation on the part of the seller to perform any aspect of the loading operation which is the seller's responsibility (*Kronos Worldwide Ltd v Sempra Oil Trading Sarl* [2004] EWCA Civ 3; [2004] C.L.C. 136 at [19], *per* Mance L.J.).

(v) *The Relationship of Banker and Seller*

The autonomy of an irrevocable credit

[Insert in line 6 of note 1307, after reference to Bank of Credit and Commerce v Somali Bank: page [478]]

34–486

Marconi Communications International Ltd v Pt Pan Indonesia Bank Ltd TBK [2004] EWHC 129 (Comm);

[Amend note 1308:]
Delete the second sentence of this note.

Illegality

[Add to the text at the end of paragraph: page [478]]

34–487

The illegality exception to the autonomy doctrine is not confined to cases where payment of the credit infringes exchange control provisions. In *Group Josi Re v Walbrook Insurance Co Ltd*,[1310a] Staughton L.J. expressed the view that a court would restrain a bank from paying under a letter of credit being used as a means of payment of an illegal arms sale, at least where the illegality was clearly established and known to the bank. More recently, in *Mahonia Ltd v JP Morgan Chase Bank*,[1310b] Colman J. refused to strike out an illegality defence to enforcement of a letter of credit where the underlying contract was alleged to have been made for an illegal purpose, namely the contravention of US Securities law.

[1310a] [1996] 1 W.L.R. 1152.
[1310b] [2003] EWHC 1927 (Comm); [2003] 2 Lloyd's Rep. 911. It was later held at the trial of the action that there was no illegality which affected the transaction: *Mahonia Ltd v JP Morgan Chase Bank* [2004] EWHC 1938 (Comm).

Ambit of rule

[Insert in note 1315, at end of second sentence, line 5: page [479]]

34–489

Balfour Beatty Civil Engineering v Technical & General Guarantee Co Ltd (1999) 68 Con. L.R. 180, 190–191; *TTI Team Telecom International Ltd v Hutchison 3G UK Ltd* [2003] EWHC 762 (TCC.); [2003] 1 All E.R. (Comm.) 914.

[Add to note 1320 at the end: page [480]]
For a critique, see Hooley, [2002] C.L.J. 279. The Singapore Court of Appeal has since recognised a separate "nullity" defence: *Beam Technology (Mfg) Pte Ltd v Standard Chartered Bank* [2003] 1 S.L.R. 597, noted by Chin and Wong, [2004] L.M.C.L.Q. 14.

Tender by third party

[Add to note 1324 at the end: page [480]]

34–490

In *Armlea plc v Gov & Co of the Bank of Scotland* (unreported, June 4, 2004), Lord Mackay (at [39]–[43]), sitting in the Outer House of the Court of Session, rejected a submission by a principal that it did not have to plead fraud when seeking an injunction against the bank to restrain payment under a demand guarantee (as opposed to where the bank wishes to avoid making payment, when fraud must be pleaded). Lord Mackay (at [44]–[46]) also rejected a submission that the fraud exception only applies to demand guarantees involved in international commerce but not to those involved in domestic commerce.

[Add new paragraphs 34–491A and 34–491B: page [481]]

34–491A **Restrictions on beneficiary's right to call for payment.** In *Sirius International Insurance Corp (Publ) v FAI General Insurance Co Ltd*,[1326a] the Court of Appeal held that the principle of autonomy did not mean that a beneficiary could draw on a letter of credit when he had expressly agreed not to do so unless certain conditions were satisfied and those conditions had not been met. In this case, the restrictions were contained in a separate agreement made between the beneficiary (Sirius) and the applicant (FAI). May L.J. stated that "although those restrictions were not terms of the letter of credit, and although the bank would have been obliged and entitled to honour a request to pay which fulfilled its terms, that does not mean that, as between themselves and FAI, Sirius were entitled to draw on the letter of credit if the express conditions of this underlying agreement were not fulfilled. They were not so entitled".[1326b] The Court of Appeal was also of the opinion that if draw-down was attempted in these circumstances, a court would be likely to grant an injunction restraining the beneficiary from drawing on the letter of credit in breach of express conditions contained in the underlying agreement. It should be noted that fraud was not alleged against Sirius and so the case does not fall within the fraud exception to the autonomy principle.

34–491B The *Sirius* case raises important questions about the extent of the autonomy principle. There must be some concern as to how far it undermines the principle and its consequential benefits of commercial certainty. However, the English courts have not shown themselves willing to embrace the wider principle of "unconscionable demand" which has gained judicial support in Australia[1326c] and Singapore.[1326d] It is not entirely clear what constitutes unconscionablity, although it seems to be something more than unfairness and less than fraud, nor as to the standard of proof required to obtain injunctive relief on this ground.[1326e] The uncertainty that this creates is obvious. Nevertheless, there have been recent dicta which suggests that the current reluctance of the English courts to apply a concept of "unconsionability" may not last forever.[1326f]

[1326a] [2003] EWCA Civ 470; [2003] 1 All E.R. (Comm.) 865, noted by Hare, [2004] C.L.J. 288. For examples of Australian cases to similar effect, see *Selvas Pty Ltd v Hansen Yuncken (SA) Pty Ltd* (1987) 6 Australian Construction Law Rep 36; *Boral Formwork v Action Motors* [2002] N.S.W.S.C. 713.

[1326b] [2003] EWCA Civ 470 at [27].

[1326c] See, *e.g. Olex Focas Pty Ltd v Skodaexport Co Ltd* [1998] 3 V.R. 380, where statute brought the concept into play.

[1326d] See, *e.g. Samwoh Asphalt Premix Pte Ltd v Sum Cheong Piling Pte Ltd* [2002] B.L.R. 459; *McConnell Dowell Construction (Aust) Pty Ltd v Semcorp Engineering and Constructions Pte Ltd* [2002] B.L.R. 450.

[1326e] See Ganotaki, [2004] L.M.C.L.Q. 148 at 152.

[1326f] See, especially, the dicta of Potter L.J. in *Montrod Ltd v Grundkotter Fleischvertriebs* [2001] EWCA Civ 1954; [2002] 1 All E.R. (Comm.) 257 at [59], and also that of Judge Thornton Q.C., sitting as a deputy High Court judge, in *TTI Team Telecom International Ltd v Hutchison 3G UK Ltd* [2003] EWHC 762 (TCC); [2003] 1 All E.R. (Comm.) 914 at [37].

CHAPTER 35

CARRIAGE BY AIR

1. INTRODUCTION

The Warsaw Convention 1929

35–002 [*Replace from "When that Act" on line 7 of page* [500] *to end of para.35–002, and notes 5 and 6, with the following*]

The unamended Warsaw Convention continues to have effect as Sch.2 to the Carriage by Air Acts (Application of Provisions) Order 2004.[5] Schedule 3 to the same Order gives effect to Montreal Additional Protocol No. 1 of 1975. The two Schedules differ only in respect of the currency units by reference to which liability limits are prescribed.

[5] SI 2004/1899.

The Montreal Convention 1999

35–006 [*In note 17, delete "(not yet in force)" and substitute: page* [502]]
, which came into force on June 28, 2004

European Council Regulation No. 2027/97

35–007— [*Pages* [502]–[503]]
35–010 The Montreal Convention 1999 came into force for the European Community on June 28, 2004, and Council Regulation No.2027/97 was radically amended, and in effect replaced, by European Parliament and Council Regulation No.889/2002, as to which see paras 35–011 *et seq*. The Air Carrier Liability

Order 1998, giving effect to Council Regulation No.2027/98 was revoked with effect from the same date by the Air Carrier Liability Regulations 2004 (SI 2004/1418).

European Parliament and Council Regulation No. 889/2002

[For the second sentence of paragraph substitute: page [503]]   **35–011**
The amending Regulation applied from June 28, 2004, the date on which the Montreal Convention entered into force for the European Community; the necessary changes to the law of the United Kingdom were made by the Air Carrier Liability Regulations 2004[34a] and the Air Carrier Liability (No. 2) Regulations 2004.[34b]

[34a] SI 2004/1418.
[34b] SI 2004/1974.

Conditions of carriage

[Add at the end of paragraph: page [504]]   **35–014**
Failure to comply with the requirements of Art.3a or Art.6 of the amended Regulation is made an offence by the Air Carrier Liability Order 2004.[39a]

[39a] SI 2004/1418.

Parties to the Conventions

[For the first sentence of note 40 substitute: page [505]]   **35–015**
s.2(1) as amended by SI 1999/213 and SI 2002/263 (and see the Carriage by Air Acts (Application of Provisions) Order 2004 (SI 2004/1899), Arts 5(2) and 6(2)).

Scope of the Conventions

[For note 43 substitute: page [page 505]]   **35–016**
Carriage by Air Acts (Application of Provisions) Order 2004 (SI 2004/1899), art.8 (excluding, in art.8(2), cases where members of the Armed Forces are carried during a time of actual or imminent hostilities, severe international tension, or great national emergency).

[For the reference to the 1967 Order at the end of paragraph, and note 44, substitute]
Sch.1 to the Carriage by Air Acts (Application of Provisions) Order 2004, under art.2(2) of which the carrier is liable only to the relevant postal administration and in accordance with the rules applicable to the relationship between carriers and postal administrations.[44]

[44] Carriage by Air Acts (Application of Provisions) Order 2004 (SI 2004/1899), art.4.

Interpretation of the Convention

[Note 48: page [506]]   **35–020**
SI 2002/263 is now in force.

[*For note 49 substitute:*]
⁴⁹ Carriage by Air Acts (Application of Provisions) Order 2004 (SI 2004/1899), arts 5(1) and 6(1).

2. INTERNATIONAL CARRIAGE

(a) *General*

Definition

35–021   [*Note 57: page* [507]]
SI 2002/263 is now in force.

[*For notes 59 and 60 substitute: page* [508]]
⁵⁹ Carriage by Air Acts (Application of Provisions) Order 2004 (SI 2004/1899), Sch.2, art.1(2); Carriage by Air Act 1961, Sch.1, art.1(2), Sch.1A as inserted by SI 1999/1312, art.1(2), Sch.1B as inserted by SI 2002/263, art.1(2).
⁶⁰ Carriage by Air Acts (Application of Provisions) Order 2004 (SI 2004/1899), Sch.2, art.1(3); Carriage by Air Act 1961, Sch.1, art.1(3), Sch.1A as inserted by SI 1999/1312, art.1(3), Sch.1B as inserted by SI 2002/263, art.1(3).

Conventions provide exclusive cause of action

35–022   [*For note 62 substitute: page* [509]]
⁶² Carriage by Air Acts (Application of Provisions) Order 2004 (SI 2004/1899), Sch.2, art.24(1); Carriage by Air Act 1961, Sch.1, art.24(1)(2), Sch.1A as inserted by SI 1999/1312, art.24(1)(2) (using different language), Sch.1B as inserted by SI 2002/263, art.29.

Jurisdiction

35–024   [*For the first sentence of note 69 substitute: page* [510]]
Carriage by Air Acts (Application of Provisions) Order 2004 (SI 2004/1899), Sch.2, art.28(1); Carriage by Air Act 1961, Sch.1, art.28(1), Sch.1A as inserted by SI 1999/1312, art.28(1).

[*Note 70*]
SI 2002/263 is now in force.

35–025   [*For the citations in the first sentence of note 71 substitute:*]
Carriage by Air Acts (Application of Provisions) Order 2004 (SI 2004/1899), Sch.2, art.28(2); Carriage by Air Act 1961, Sch.1, art.28(2), Sch.1A as inserted by SI 1999/1312, art.28(2), Sch.1B as inserted by SI 2002/263, art.33(4).

Limitation of actions

35–026   [*For note 82 substitute: page* [511]]
⁸² Carriage by Air Acts (Application of Provisions) Order 2004 (SI 2004/1899), Sch.2, art.29(1); Carriage by Air Act 1961, Sch.1, art.29(1), Sch.1A as inserted by SI 1999/1312, art.29(1), Sch.1B as inserted by SI 2002/263, art.35(1). English law will, as the *lex fori*, determine the method of calculating the period of limitation: Carriage by Air Acts (Application of Provisions) Order 2004 (SI

2004/1899), Sch.2, art.29(2); Carriage by Air Act 1961, Sch.1, art.29(2), Sch.1A as inserted by SI 1999/1312, art.29(2), Sch.1B as inserted by SI 2002/263, art.35(2).

(b) *Passengers*

Passenger ticket

[*For note 93 substitute: page* [513]]
[93] Carriage by Air Acts (Application of Provisions) Order 2004 (SI 2004/1899), Sch.2, art.3(1).

35–028

[*Note 95*]
SI 2002/263 is now in force.

Absence, irregularity or loss of passenger ticket

[*For the first line of note 103 substitute: page* [514]]
Carriage by Air Acts (Application of Provisions) Order 2004 (SI 2004/1899), Sch.2, art.3(2).

35–030

[*Note 106*]
SI 2002/263 is now in force.

[*For note 107 substitute:*]
[107] Carriage by Air Act 1961, Sch.1, art.34, Sch.1A as inserted by SI 1999/1312, art.34, Sch.1B as inserted by SI 2002/263, art.51. The Warsaw Convention 1929 is wholly excluded in such cases: Carriage by Air Acts (Application of Provisions) Order 2004 (SI 2004/1899), Sch.2, art.34.

Right of refusal

[*For the first sentence of note 108 substitute: page* [514]]
Carriage by Air Acts (Application of Provisions) Order 2004 (SI 2004/1899), Sch.2, art.33; Carriage by Air Act 1961, Sch.1, art.33, Sch.1A as inserted by SI 1999/1312, art.33, Sch.1B as inserted by SI 2002/263, art.27.

35–031

Liability for death and bodily injury

[*For note 111 substitute: page* 515]]
[111] Carriage by Air Acts (Application of Provisions) Order 2004 (SI 2004/1899), Sch.2, art.17.

35–032

[*Note 112*]
SI 2002/263 is now in force.

"Accident"

[*Page* [516]]
The United States Supreme Court has held that an omission may be treated as an accident; there is no requirement of a positive action on anyone's part: *Olympic Airways v Husain* 124 S Ct 1221 (2004), pet. for rehearing denied 124 S Ct 2065 (2004). *cf. Deep Vein Thrombosis and Air Travel Group Litigation* [2003] EWCA Civ 1005; [2004] QB 234, where Lord Phillips of Worth

35–033

Matravers MR advances the contrary view. In *Olympic Airways v Husain*, the deceased passenger had been refused a change of seat to avoid the cigarette smoke to which he was allergic; this was an unusual event external to the passenger and so an "accident".

"Bodily injury"

35–034   *[Page [516]]*
There is no liability for mental injuries which are accompanied by, but not caused by physical injuries: *Ehrlich v American Airlines Inc* 360 F 3d 366 (2nd Cir, 2004).

Defences available to the carrier: "all necessary measures"

35–035   *[For the first line of note 124 substitute:]*
Carriage by Air Acts (Application of Provisions) Order 2004 (SI 2004/1899), Sch.2, art.20(1);

[Delete second sentence and note 125: page [517]]
European Council Regulation No.2027/97 was radically amended, and in effect replaced, by European Parliament and Council Regulation No.889/2002, as to which see paras 35–011 *et seq*. The Air Carrier Liability Order 1998 was revoked with effect from the same date by the Air Carrier Liability Regulations 2004 (SI 2004/1418). Community air carriers now fall within the regime of the Montreal Convention 1999.

[Note 126]
SI 2002/263 is now in force.

Contributory negligence

35–036   *[Page [518]]*
European Council Regulation No.2027/97 was radically amended, and in effect replaced, by European Parliament and Council Regulation No.889/2002, as to which see paras 35–011 *et seq*. Community air carriers now fall within the regime of the Montreal Convention 1999.

[For note 135 substitute:]
[135] Carriage by Air Acts (Application of Provisions) Order 2004 (SI 2004/1899), Sch.2, art.21.

[Note 138]
SI 2002/263 is now in force.

Upper financial limit of liability

35–037   *[Page [518]]*
European Council Regulation No.2027/97 was radically amended, and in effect replaced, by European Parliament and Council Regulation No.889/2002, as to which see paras 35–011 *et seq*. Community air carriers now fall within the regime of the Montreal Convention 1999.

[*For note 141 substitute:*]
¹⁴¹ Carriage by Air Acts (Application of Provisions) Order 2004 (SI 2004/1899), Sch.2, art.22.

[*Note 145; page* [519]]
SI 2002/263 is now in force.

Misconduct

[*For the first sentence of note 149 substitute: page* [520]]
Carriage by Air Acts (Application of Provisions) Order 2004 (SI 2004/1899), Sch.2, art.25.

35–039

[*Note 152*]
SI 2002/263 is now in force.

Fatal Accidents

[*Note 161: page* [522]]
SI 2002/263 is now in force.

35–045

Several Actions by one passenger

[*Notes 164, 167, 168 and 169: pages* [522]–[523]]
SI 2002/263 is now in force.

35–046

[*In line 7: page* [522]]
The reference in the text to note 165 should now be to the Carriage by Air Acts (Application of Provisions) Order 2004.

[*For note 165 substitute:*]
¹⁶⁵ SI 2004/1899, art.7.

Overbooking

[*Last sentence, text to note 172: page* [523]]
Council Regulation 295/91 is with effect from February 17, 2005, repealed and replaced by European Parliament and Council Regulation No.261/2004 of February 11, 2004, for the text of which see OJ 2004 L46/1.

35–047

Successive carriers

[*For the first sentence of note 173 substitute: page* [524]]
Carriage by Air Acts (Application of Provisions) Order 2004 (SI 2004/1899), Sch.2, art.1(3); Carriage by Air Act 1961, Sch.1, art.1(3), Sch.1A as inserted by SI 1999/1312, art.1(3), Sch.1B as inserted by SI 2002/263, art.1(3).

35–048

[*For the first sentence of note 174 substitute:*]
Carriage by Air Acts (Application of Provisions) Order 2004 (SI 2004/1899), Sch.2, art.30(1); Carriage by Air Act 1961, Sch.1, art.30(1), Sch.1A as inserted by SI 1999/1312, art.30(1), Sch.1B as inserted by SI 2002/263, art.36(1).

[*For note 175 substitute:*]
Carriage by Air Acts (Application of Provisions) Order 2004 (SI 2004/1899), Sch.2, art.30(2); Carriage by Air Act 1961, Sch.1, art.30(2), Sch.1A as inserted by SI 1999/1312, art.30(2), Sch.1B as inserted by SI 2002/263, art.36(2).

Contracting carriers and "actual" carriers

35–049   [*Note 178: page* [525]]
SI 2002/263 is now in force.

(c) *Baggage*

Forms of baggage

35–052   [*For the first line of note 186 substitute: page* [526]]
Carriage by Air Acts (Application of Provisions) Order 2004 (SI 2004/1899), Sch.2, art.22(3);

[*Note 186, line 4*]
SI 2002/263 is now in force.

Baggage check

35–053   [*For note 189 substitute: page* [526]]
[189] Carriage by Air Acts (Application of Provisions) Order 2004 (SI 2004/1899), Sch.2, art.4.

[*For note 191 substitute:*]
[191] Carriage by Air Acts (Application of Provisions) Order 2004 (SI 2004/1899), Sch.2, art.4(4).

[*Note 195: page* [527]]
SI 2002/263 is now in force.

Liability for damage, destruction or loss

35–054   [*Page* [527]]
Under European Parliament and Council Regulation No.889/2002, Community air carriers now fall within the regime of the Montreal Convention 1999.

[*For the first line of note 196 substitute:*]
Carriage by Air Acts (Application of Provisions) Order 2004 (SI 2004/1899), Sch.2, art.18(1);

[*For the first line of note 197 substitute:*]
Carriage by Air Acts (Application of Provisions) Order 2004 (SI 2004/1899), Sch.2, art.18(2);

[*Note 198: page* [528]]
SI 2002/263 is now in force.

[Page [528]]
[For note 200 substitute:]
²⁰⁰ Carriage by Air Acts (Application of Provisions) Order 2004 (SI 2004/1899), Sch.2, art.22(2).

[For note 202 substitute:]
²⁰² Carriage by Air Acts (Application of Provisions) Order 2004 (SI 2004/1899), Sch.2, art.22(3).

[In note 205, line 1, for the citation of the 1967 Order substitute:]
Carriage by Air Acts (Application of Provisions) Order 2004 (SI 2004/1899), Sch.3, art.22(2)(3).

[Note 206]
SI 2002/263 is now in force.

[For note 207 substitute: page [529]]
²⁰⁷ Carriage by Air Acts (Application of Provisions) Order 2004 (SI 2004/1899), Sch.2, art.22(2); Carriage by Air Act 1961, Sch.1, art.22(2)(*a*), Sch.1A as inserted by SI 1999/1312, art.22(2)(*a*), Sch.1B as inserted by SI 2002/263, art.22(2).

Time for making claims

[For notes 208 to 210 substitute: page [529]]
²⁰⁸ Carriage by Air Acts (Application of Provisions) Order 2004 (SI 2004/1899), Sch.2, art.26(2); Carriage by Air Act 1961, Sch.1, art.26(2), Sch.1A as inserted by SI 1999/1312, art.26(2), Sch.1B as inserted by SI 2002/263, art.31(2).
²⁰⁹ Carriage by Air Acts (Application of Provisions) Order 2004 (SI 2004/1899), Sch.2, art.35; Carriage by Air Act 1961, Sch.1, art.35, Sch.1A as inserted by SI 1999/1312, art.35, Sch.1B as inserted by SI 2002/263, art.52.
²¹⁰ Carriage by Air Acts (Application of Provisions) Order 2004 (SI 2004/1899), Sch.2, art.26(4); Carriage by Air Act 1961, Sch.1, art.26(4), Sch.1A as inserted by SI 1999/1312, art.26(4), Sch.1B as inserted by SI 2002/263, art.31(4).

(d) *Cargo*

Air waybill

[For notes 211 to 215 substitute: page [529]]
²¹¹ Carriage by Air Acts (Application of Provisions) Order 2004 (SI 2004/1899), Sch.2, art.5(1); Carriage by Air Act 1961, Sch.1, art.5(1).
²¹² Carriage by Air Acts (Application of Provisions) Order 2004 (SI 2004/1899), Sch.2, art.10(1); Carriage by Air Act 1961, Sch.1, art.10(1).
²¹³ Carriage by Air Acts (Application of Provisions) Order 2004 (SI 2004/1899), Sch.2, art.6(5); Carriage by Air Act 1961, Sch.1, art.6(5).
²¹⁴ Carriage by Air Acts (Application of Provisions) Order 2004 (SI 2004/1899), Sch.2, art.7; Carriage by Air Act 1961, Sch.1, art.7.
²¹⁵ Carriage by Air Acts (Application of Provisions) Order 2004 (SI 2004/1899), Sch.2, art.6(1)(2); Carriage by Air Act 1961, Sch.1, art.6(1)(2).

Statements in waybill

[For note 217 substitute: page [530]]
²¹⁷ Carriage by Air Acts (Application of Provisions) Order 2004 (SI 2004/1899), Sch.2, art.11(2); Carriage by Air Act 1961, Sch.1, art.11(2).

Absence of waybill, etc.

35–059   [*For the first line of note 219 substitute: page* [530]]
Carriage by Air Acts (Application of Provisions) Order 2004 (SI 2004/1899), Sch.2, art.9;

Cargo documentation under recent conventions

35–060   [*Notes 223 and 224: page* [530]]
SI 2002/263 is now in force.

Acceptability of goods for carriage

35–061   [*Note 226: page* [*531*]]
Amend the citation to CSC(24)1601.

[*Note 227*]
Amend the citation to art.3.1.1.2.

Liability for damage, destruction or loss

35–062   [*For the first line of note 231 substitute: page* [531]]
Carriage by Air Acts (Application of Provisions) Order 2004 (SI 2004/1899), Sch.2, art.18(1);

[*For the first line of note 232 substitute:*]
Carriage by Air Acts (Application of Provisions) Order 2004 (SI 2004/1899), Sch.2, art.18(2);

[*Note 234: page* [532]]
SI 2002/263 is now in force.

Upper financial limit of liability

35–063   [*For notes 239 and 240 substitute: page* [532]]
[239] Carriage by Air Acts (Application of Provisions) Order 2004 (SI 2004/1899), Sch.2, art.22(2); Carriage by Air Act 1961, Sch.1, art.22(2)(3) (as amended by the Carriage by Air and Road Act 1979, s.4), Sch.1A as inserted by SI 1999/1312, art.22(2)(*a*), Sch.1B as inserted by SI 2002/263, art.22(2).
[240] Carriage by Air Acts (Application of Provisions) Order 2004 (SI 2004/1899), Sch.2, art.22(2); Carriage by Air Act 1961, Sch.1, art.22(2)(*a*), Sch.1A as inserted by SI 1999/1312, art.22(2)(*a*), Sch.1B as inserted by SI 2002/263, art.22(2).

Stoppage in transit

35–064   [*For note 243 substitute: page* [533]]
[243] Carriage by Air Acts (Application of Provisions) Order 2004 (SI 2004/1899), Sch.2, arts 12(4), 13(1); Carriage by Air Act 1961, Sch.1, arts 12(4), 13(1), Sch.1A as inserted by SI 1999/1312, arts 12(4), 13(1), Sch.1B as inserted by SI 2002/263, arts 12(4), 13(1).

[For the first sentence of note 244 substitute:]
Carriage by Air Acts (Application of Provisions) Order 2004 (SI 2004/1899), Sch.2, art.12(1); Carriage by Air Act 1961, Sch.1, art.12(1), Sch.1A as inserted by SI 1999/1312, art.12(1), Sch.1B as inserted by SI 2002/263, art.12(1).

[For the first sentence of note 245 substitute:]
Carriage by Air Acts (Application of Provisions) Order 2004 (SI 2004/1899), Sch.2, art.12(2); Carriage by Air Act 1961, Sch.1, art.12(2), Sch.1A as inserted by SI 1999/1312, art.12(2), Sch.1B as inserted by SI 2002/263, art.12(2).

[For note 246 substitute]
[246] Carriage by Air Acts (Application of Provisions) Order 2004 (SI 2004/1899), Sch.2, arts 12(4), 13(1); Carriage by Air Act 1961, Sch.1, arts 12(4), 13(1), Sch.1A as inserted by SI 1999/1312, arts 12(4), 13(1), Sch.1B as inserted by SI 2002/263, arts 12(4), 13(1).

Delivery to the consignee

[For notes 247 to 249 substitute: page [533]]   **35–065**
[247] Carriage by Air Acts (Application of Provisions) Order 2004 (SI 2004/1899), Sch.2, art.13(2); Carriage by Air Act 1961, Sch.1, art.13(2), Sch.1A as inserted by SI 1999/1312, art.13(2), Sch.1B as inserted by SI 2002/263, art.13(2). See the I.A.T.A. recommended Conditions of Carriage (CSC(24)1601), art.8.1.
[248] Carriage by Air Acts (Application of Provisions) Order 2004 (SI 2004/1899), Sch.2, art.13(1); Carriage by Air Act 1961, Sch.1, art.13(1), Sch.1A as inserted by SI 1999/1312, art.13(1), Sch.1B as inserted by SI 2002/263, art.13(1).
[249] CSC(24)1601, art.8.3.

Time for making claims: damage or delay

[For the first sentence of note 254 substitute: page [534]]   **35–067**
Carriage by Air Acts (Application of Provisions) Order 2004 (SI 2004/1899), Sch.2, art.26(2); Carriage by Air Act 1961, Sch.1, art.26(2), Sch.1A as inserted by SI 1999/1312, art.26(2), Sch.1B as inserted by SI 2002/263, art.31(2).

[For notes 255 and 256 substitute:]
[255] Carriage by Air Acts (Application of Provisions) Order 2004 (SI 2004/1899), Sch.2, art.35; Carriage by Air Act 1961, Sch.1, art.35, Sch.1A as inserted by SI 1999/1312, art.35, Sch.1B as inserted by SI 2002/263, art.52.
[256] Carriage by Air Acts (Application of Provisions) Order 2004 (SI 2004/1899), Sch.2, art.26(4); Carriage by Air Act 1961, Sch.1, art.26(4), Sch.1A as inserted by SI 1999/1312, art.26(4), Sch.1B as inserted by SI 2002/263, art.31(4).

Loss of cargo

[For the first sentence of note 257 substitute: page [535]]   **35–068**
Carriage by Air Acts (Application of Provisions) Order 2004 (SI 2004/1899), Sch.2, art.23; Carriage by Air Act 1961, Sch.1, art.23, Sch.1A as inserted by SI 1999/1312, art.23, Sch.1B as inserted by SI 2002/263, art.26.

[Note 257, last line]
SI 2002/263 is now in force.

[For the first sentence of note 258 substitute:]
Carriage by Air Acts (Application of Provisions) Order 2004 (SI 2004/1899), Sch.2, art.13(3); Carriage by Air Act 1961, Sch.1, art.13(3), Sch.1A as inserted by SI 1999/1312, art.13(3), Sch.1B as inserted by SI 2002/263, art.13(3).

Who can sue the carrier

35–069   *[For the first sentence of note 264 substitute: page [535]]*
Carriage by Air Acts (Application of Provisions) Order 2004 (SI 2004/1899), Sch.2, arts 13(3) and 24(1); Carriage by Air Act 1961, Sch.1, arts 13(3) and 24(1), Sch.1A as inserted by SI 1999/1312, arts 13(3) and 24(1), Sch.1B as inserted by SI 2002/263, arts 13(3) and 29.

35–070   *[For notes 266 and 267 substitute:]*
[266] Carriage by Air Acts (Application of Provisions) Order 2004 (SI 2004/1899), Sch.2, art.24(1); Carriage by Air Act 1961, Sch.1, art.24(1), Sch.1A as inserted by SI 1999/1312, art.24(1), Sch.1B as inserted by SI 2002/263, art.29.
[267] Carriage by Air Acts (Application of Provisions) Order 2004 (SI 2004/1899), Sch.2, art.24(2); Carriage by Air Act 1961, Sch.1, art.24(2), Sch.1A as inserted by SI 1999/1312, art.24(2), Sch.1B as inserted by SI 2002/263, art.29.

(e) *Delay to passengers, baggage or cargo*

Liability for delay

35–072   *[For notes 275 to 278 substitute: page [537]]*
[275] Carriage by Air Acts (Application of Provisions) Order 2004 (SI 2004/1899), Sch.2, art.19; Carriage by Air Act 1961, Sch.1, art.19, Sch.1A as inserted by SI 1999/1312, art.19, Sch.1B as inserted by SI 2002/263, art.19.
[276] Carriage by Air Acts (Application of Provisions) Order 2004 (SI 2004/1899), Sch.2, art.20; Carriage by Air Act 1961, Sch.1, art.20, Sch.1A as inserted by SI 1999/1312, art.20, Sch.1B as inserted by SI 2002/263, art.19.
[277] Carriage by Air Acts (Application of Provisions) Order 2004 (SI 2004/1899), Sch.2, art.20(2).
[278] Carriage by Air Acts (Application of Provisions) Order 2004 (SI 2004/1899), Sch.2, art.21; Carriage by Air Act 1961, Sch.1, art.21, Sch.1A as inserted by SI 1999/1312, art.21, Sch.1B as inserted by SI 2002/263, art.20.

[For note 281 substitute:]
[281] See I.A.T.A. recommended Conditions (PSC(24) 1724), Art.9.1.1.

3. NON-INTERNATIONAL CARRIAGE

Applicable rules

35–073   *[Substitute new paragraph: pages [537]–[538]]*
Applicable rules. The Conventions treated above regulate only international carriage. Carriage which is not international carriage as defined in any of the Conventions falls outside the Convention system. The applicable law is to be found in two sources. Community air carriers engaged in the carriage of persons

or baggage are subject to European Parliament and Council Regulation No.889/2002,[282] which applies to national as well as international carriage. The liability of other air carriers, and Community air carriers engaged in the carriage of cargo, is governed by Schedule 1 to the Carriage by Air Acts (Application of Provisions) Order 2004,[283] which applies a modified version of the Montreal Convention 1999. Subject to the Regulation, the 2004 Order applies to all carriage by air other than carriage to which the Warsaw-Hague text, the MP4 Convention or the Montreal Convention 1999 applies, and Sch.1 applies to carriage which is not international carriage as defined in Schs 2 or 3 (applying the original Warsaw Convention and that Convention as amended by Montreal Additional protocol No.1 of 1975).[283a] To avoid giving too extensive a scope to the predecessor provisions, for it was arguable that the provisions of the United Kingdom Order applied to internal carriage in other countries, the House of Lords held that their application is limited to (a) carriage in which the places of departure and destination and any agreed stopping places are all within the United Kingdom or other British territory; and (b) non-convention carriage involving a place of departure or destination or an agreed stopping place in a foreign state and a place of departure or destination or an agreed stopping place in the United Kingdom or other British territory.[284]

[282] See paras 35–011 *et seq.*
[283] SI 2004/1899. Note that art.2 is amended by SI 2004/1974.
[283a] Carriage by Air Acts (Application of Provisions) Order 2004 (SI 2004/1899), arts 3(1) and 4.
[284] *Holmes v Bangladesh Biman Corp.* [1989] A.C. 1112.

The modified convention regime under Schedule 1 to the 1967 Order

[Substitute new paragraph: page [538]]   35–074
   The modified convention regime under Schedule 1 to the 2004 Order. Only parts of the Montreal Convention 1999 are applied by the 2004 Order.[285] Chapter II (Arts 3–16) dealing with documentation is omitted except for parts of Art.3 requiring the carrier to deliver a baggage identification tag for each piece of checked baggage. Liability for death or injury is unlimited but if the carrier proves an absence of fault there is no liability beyond 100,000 SDRs.[286] There are no provisions regulating the carriage of mail and postal packages save for a provision that in these cases the carrier is liable only to the relevant postal administration and in accordance with the rules applicable to the relationship between carriers and postal administrations.[287]

[285] Carriage by Air Acts (Application of Provisions) Order 2004 (SI 2004/1899).
[286] *Ibid.*, Sch.1, art.21.
[287] *Ibid.*, Sch.1, art.2(2). See the Postal Services Act 2000, s.90; *American Express Co v British Airways Board* [1983] 1 W.L.R. 701; *Post Office v British World Airlines Ltd* [2000] 1 All E.R. (Comm.) 532.

CHAPTER 36

CARRIAGE BY LAND

2. INTERNAL CARRIAGE

(a) *Goods*

(iv) *Contractual Liability*

Construction of contracts

36–028   [*Add to note 133 after second sentence: page* [553]]
    In *Frans Maas (UK) Ltd v Samsung Electronics (UK) Ltd* [2004] EWHC 1502 (Comm); [2004] All E.R. (D) 362, the court held that the limitation provision under the BIFA Conditions was reasonable.

(v) *Liability in Tort*

Liability in tort

[*Add to the end of note 258: page* [565]]
As to the employer's vicarious liability for the acts of his employees, see
Frans Maas (UK) Ltd v Samsung Electronics (UK) Ltd [2004] EWHC 1502
(Comm); [2004] All E.R. (D) 362.

3. INTERNATIONAL CARRIAGE

(a) *Introduction*

Convention for Carriage of Passengers and Luggage by Road

[*Delete the fourth to eighth sentences and substitute: pages* [586]–[587]]
The possibility of signature and ratification grows remote, however, given that
the United Kingdom's implementing legislation in respect of the CVR (the
Carriage of Passengers by Road Act 1974) was repealed by the Statute Law
(Repeals) Act 2004, s.1(1) and Sch.1, Pt 14.

Chapter 37

CONSTRUCTION CONTRACTS

2. FORMATION OF CONTRACT

(a) General Principles

General principles

[Add to note 95, page [653]]   **37–039**
   See *Ove Arup & Partners International Ltd v Mirant Asia-Pacific Construction (Hong Kong) Ltd* [2003] EWCA Civ 1729; [2004] B.L.R. 49.

3. CONTRACT TERMS

(b) Contract Documents

Incorporated documents

[Page [666]]   **37–064**
   See the approach of the Court of Appeal in *Aqua Design Ltd v Kier Regional Ltd* [2002] EWCA Civ 797; [2003] B.L.R. 111 to the question of whether certain provisions of the Standard DOM/1 Form of Sub-Contract were incorporated into a negotiated sub-contract.

(d) Statutes Relevant to Construction

Statutory implied terms

37–077   [*Add to end of note 221: page* [671]]
Contracts for the supply of materials are normally governed by the Sale of Goods Act 1979 (see Main Work, Vol. II, Chap.43); see *Jewsons Ltd v Boykan* [2003] EWCA Civ 1030; [2004] B.L.R. 31 on fitness for purpose under s.14(3) in the building context.

4. PARTICULAR FEATURES

(b) Instructions, Certificates and Approval

Final certificate

37–101   [*Add to note 337: page* [684]]
See *Cantrell v Wright and Fuller Ltd* [2003] EWHC 1545 (TCC); [2003] B.L.R. 412

6. SUB-CONTRACTS

(a) Sub-Contractors

No right to direct payment

37–169   [*Add at end of paragraph: page* [712]]
In each case, it is a question of construction of the contract as to what rights and obligations have been conferred, or imposed, on the parties.[543a]

[543a] *Actionstrength Ltd v International Glass Engineering IN.GL.EN SpA* [2003] UKHL 17; [2003] 2 A.C. 541 and *Brican Fabrications Ltd v Merchant City Developments Ltd* [2003] B.L.R. 512 (Court of Session).

10. DISPUTES

(d) Litigation

Presentation of claims

37–254   [*Add to note 772: page* [747]]
See the recent review of the decided cases on "global" claims by Lord Macfayden in *John Doyle Construction Ltd v Laing Management (Scotland) Ltd* [2002] B.L.R. 393 (Court of Session).

[Add new paragraph: page [747]]

Alternative dispute resolution (ADR). Where a commercial agreement **37–254A**
between parties requires ADR to be undertaken, then the strong tendency of the
courts, especially in the specialist divisions, is to refuse to permit a party to
proceedings without having instituted ADR proceedings first.[778a]

[778a] *Cable & Wireless plc v IBM UK Ltd* [2002] EWHC 2059 (Comm); [2003] B.L.R. 89.

CHAPTER 38

CREDIT AND SECURITY

1. THE CONSUMER CREDIT ACT 1974

Regulations, orders etc

[*Add at end of note 18: page* [755]]
SI 2004/1481, 1482, 1483, 1484.

Banking Code

[*Page* [757]]
See also the Business Banking Code (para.34–225 of the Main Work).

Reform of consumer credit law

[*Page* [757]]
The following statutory instruments have been made: Consumer Credit (Disclosure of Information) Regulations 2004 (SI 2004/1481) (operative May 31, 2005); Consumer Credit (Agreements) (Amendment) Regulations 2004 (SI 2004/1482) (operative May 31, 2005); Consumer Credit (Early Settlement) Regulations 2004 (SI 2004/1483) (operative May 31, 2005); Consumer Credit (Advertisements) Regulations 2004 (SI 2004/1484) (operative October 31, 2004).

(a) *Terminology of the Act*

"Consumer credit agreement"

[*Add to note 52: page* [759]]
SI 1989/1125 is revoked and replaced by SI 2004/1484: see below, para. 38–061

"Credit"

[*Add to note 62: page* [759]]
Nejad v City Index Ltd [2000] C.C.L.R. 7 (C.A.) (allowing a client a "credit allocation" for future gambling did not constitute the provision of credit); *McMillan Williams v Range* [2004] EWCA Civ 294; [2004] 1 W.L.R. 1858 (payment of salary as an advance against commission did not constitute the provision of credit). It would seem that, at the time the agreement is made, it must be certain that credit will be provided: *ibid.*

"Credit-token agreement"

[*Add to note 120: page* [765]]
SI 1983/1553 is amended by SI 2004/1482; see para.38–071, below.

"Consumer hire agreement"

38–033 *[Add to note 136: page [767]]*
SI 1989/1125 is revoked and replaced by SI 2004/1484; see para.38–061 below.

"Exempt agreement"

38–037 *[Add after reference to Ketley v Gilbert in note 159: page [768]]*
Thew v Cole [2003] EWCA Civ 1828; *The Times*, January 15, 2004.

38–040 *[Add at end of note 164: page [769]]*
and by Sch.17, para.47 of the Communications Act 2003.

Consequences if part is a separate agreement

38–048 *[Add to note 212: page [772]]*
SI 1983/1553 is amended by SI 2004/1482; see para.38–071, below.

"Total change for credit"

38–055 *[Add to note 234: page [774]]*
SI 2004/1482.

(c) *Seeking Business*

Advertising and quotations

38–061 The Consumer Credit (Advertisement) Regulations 1989 are revoked and replaced by the Consumer Credit (Advertisement) Regulations 2004 (SI 2004/1484) (operative October 31, 2004).

[Delete note 294: page [778] and substitute]
SI 1999/2725, as amended by SI 2000/1797. But these regulations are revoked in part by SI 2004/1484, above.

(e) *The Agreement*

Pre-contract disclosure

38–070 *[Page [781]]*
The Consumer Credit (Disclosure of Information) Regulations 2004 (SI 2004/1481), have now been made under s.55(1) of the Act (operative May 31, 2005). These regulations do not apply to agreements to which s.58 of the Act applies (see para.38–496 of the Main Work) nor in respect of distance contracts (as defined in reg.1(2)).

Form and content of the agreement

[Page [781]]   **38–071**
The Consumer Credit (Agreements) Regulations 1983 are extensively amended by the Consumer Credit (Agreements) (Amendment) Regulations 2004 (SI 2004/1482) (operative May 31, 2005).

Signing of agreement

[Add to notes 339 and 341: page [782]]   **38–072**
SI 1983/1553 is amended by SI 2004/1482; see para.38–071, above.

[Add at end of note 347]
as amended by SI 2004/1482.

Failure to comply

[Add to note 391: page [785]]   **38–083**
SI 1983/1553 is amended by SI 2004/1482: see para.38–071, above.

(f) *Withdrawal and Cancellation*

Consumer Protection (Cancellation of Contracts Concluded away from Business Premises) Regulations 1987

[Add to note 450: page [789]]   **38–093**
See also *Heininger v Bayerische Hypo-und Vereinsbank AG* (C481/99) [2004] All E.R. (EC) 1 (mortgage transaction).

(g) *Supply of Information*

Information as to settlement figure

[Amend the text to note 642: page [802]]   **38–124**
The period of 12 days prescribed by SI 1983/1564 is reduced to seven days by SI 2004/1483, reg.9, as from May 31, 2005.

[Add to note 643]
SI 1983/1564 is amended and SI 1983/1562 revoked and replaced by SI 2004/1483; see para.38–139, below.

(h) *Variation of Agreements*

Mutual variation by subsequent agreement

[Add to note 676: page [806]]   **38–131**
SI 1983/1553 is amended by SI 2004/1482; see para.38–071, above.

Form etc., of modifying agreement

38–135   [*Add to note 688: page* [807]]
SI 1983/1553 is amended by SI 2004/1482: see para.38–071, above.

(i) *Appropriation of Payments and Early Settlement*

Rebate on early settlement etc

38–139—   [*Page* [808]]
38–140   The Consumer Credit (Rebate on Early Settlement) Regulations 1983 are revoked and replaced by the Consumer Credit (Rebate on Early Settlement) Regulations 2004 (SI 2004/1483), but the 1983 Regulations continue to apply for a limited period to regulated consumer credit agreements entered into before the date on which the 2004 Regulations come into force (May 31, 2005). The 2004 Regulations incorporate an actuarial formula for the calculation of the rebate in place of the various formulae provided for in the 1983 Regulations. Regulation 6 provides for the settlement date to be deferred by a month (or, at the option of the creditor, 30 days) in the case of agreements for a term of more than one year, and is thus less generous to the creditor than the 1983 Regulations.

(k) *Security*

"Security" defined

38–161   [*Add to note 795: page* [816]]
SI 1989/1125 is revoked and replaced by SI 2004/1484; see para.38–061, above.

Security provided by debtor or hirer

38–168   [*Add at end of note 814: page* [818]]
SI 2004/1482.

(m) *Extortionate Credit Bargains*

Rate of Interest

38–198   [*Add to note 979: page* [830]]
Batooneh v Asombang [2003] EWHC 2111 (QB) (interest rate of 100 per cent on informal commercial loan reduced to 25 per cent).

(n) *Ancillary Credit Businesses*

Seeking business

[Add to note 1076: page [839]]
SI 1989/1125 is entirely revoked, and SI 1999/2725 and SI 2000/1797 partially revoked, by SI 2004/1484 (operative October 31, 2004): see para.38–061, above.

2. LOANS AND INTEREST

(b) *Interest*

Default interest

38–258

[Add to note 1250: page [856]]
Contrast *Jeancharm Ltd v Barnet Football Club Ltd* [2003] EWCA Civ 58; [2003] 92 Const. L.R. 26 (default interest of 5 per cent per week held penal).

3. HIRE-PURCHASE AGREEMENTS

(e) *Rights and Liabilities of Third Parties*

(v) *Execution and Distress*

Execution

38–390

[Amend the text to note 1758: page [903]]
s.138B(1) of the Supreme Court Act 1981 has been repealed by s.109(3) and Sch.10 of the Courts Act 2003 and replaced by Sch.7, para.11, of that Act.

6. CREDIT AND OTHER PAYMENT CARDS AND CHECKS

"Credit token" and "credit-token agreements"

38–462

[Add to note 2003: page [924]]
SI 1983/1553 is amended by SI 2004/1482: see para.38–071, above.

8. Mortgages of Land

Form, etc

38–494   [*Page* [932]]

The Consumer Credit (Disclosure of Information) Regulations 2004 (SI 2004/1481) (see para.38–070, above) do not apply to agreements to which s.58 of the Act applies.

CHAPTER 39

EMPLOYMENT

1. Introduction

The contract of service or personally to execute any work or labour: "workers" and "persons employed"

39–009　　*[Add to note 65: page [943]]*

See *Mingeley v Pennock and Ivory* [2004] EWCA Civ 328; [2004] I.C.R. 727, where the relationship between a taxi-driver and the organisation co-ordinating his work was held not to amount to a contract personally to execute any work or labour; see also Supplement, para.39–023, n.150.

[Add to note 66]

See *South East Sheffield Citizens Advice Bureau v Grayson* [2004] I.R.L.R. 353, E.A.T., where an unpaid volunteer worker was held to fall outside this definition.

2. The Factors identifying a Contract of Employment

The extent of the obligation to work or to employ

39–023　　*[Add to note 150: page [951]]*

Compare now *Mingeley v Pennock and Ivory* [2004] EWCA Civ 328; [2004] I.C.R. 727, where the relationship between a taxi-driver and the organisation co-ordinating his work was held not to amount to a contract personally to execute any work or labour.

[Add to note 152]

Compare the decision in *Dacas v Brook Street Bureau (UK) Ltd* [2004] EWCA Civ 217; [2004] I.R.L.R. 358, regarding the relationship between the employment agency and the temporary agency worker—see further, Main Work and Supplement para.39–027, n.184.

Special cases: (2) agency workers

39–027　　*[Add to note 184: page [954]]*

However, the Court of Appeal in *Dacas v Brook Street Bureau (UK) Ltd* [2004] EWCA Civ 217; [2004] I.R.L.R. 358, held that the temporary agency worker was not an "employee" of the agency, though she might be an employee of the end-user of her services.

3. FORMATION OF THE CONTRACT

Public policy, restraint of trade, and illegality

[*Add to note 221: page* [958]]   **39–032**
The decision of the EAT was upheld by the Court of Appeal in *Vakante v
Addey & Stanhope School* [2004] EWCA Civ 1065.

[*Add to note 228*]
The approach in the *Woolston Hall Leisure* case was reiterated and applied in
Colen v Cebrian (UK) Ltd [2003] EWCA Civ 1676; [2004] I.C.R. 568.

4. COLLECTIVE AGREEMENTS AND STATUTORY AWARDS OF TERMS

(b) *Incorporation of Collective Agreements into Individual Contracts of Employment*

Incorporation by implication

[*Add to note 346: page* [970]]   **39–048**
Compare *Kaur v MG Rover Group Ltd* [2004] I.R.L.R 279, Q.B.D., where a
job security provision in a collective agreement was held to appropriate for
incorporation into individual contracts of employment.

5. RIGHTS AND DUTIES UNDER AND ASSOCIATED WITH A CONTRACT OF EMPLOYMENT

(b) *Duties of the Employer*

(ii) *Other Duties*

Action in Tort

[*Add to note 767: page* [1006]]   **39–100**
Update reference to *Clerk & Lindsell* to 18th ed., 2004.

[*Add to note 769*]
In *Barber v Somerset County Council* [2004] UKHL 13; [2004] 1 W.L.R.
1089, the House of Lords broadly endorsed the guidelines laid down in *Suther-
land v Hatton*, though applying them to somewhat different outcomes in the
particular cases which were under appeal.

The Working Time Regulations

39–108   [*Add to note 823: page* [1011]]
Compare, as to collective agreements, *Prison Service v Bewley* [2004] I.C.R. 422, E.A.T.

[*Add to note 824*]
The issue of whether this entitlement can be discharged by the payment of "rolled-up" holiday pay has been referred to the E.C.J. by the Court of Appeal in *Caulfield v Marshalls Clay Products Ltd* [2004] EWCA Civ 422; [2004] 2 C.M.L.R. 45.

Equality clauses in contracts of employment

39–122   [*Add to note 887: page* [1017]]
Compare *Allonby v Accrington & Rossendale College* Case C-256/01 [2004] I.R.L.R .224, E.C.J., as to the construction of the "same employment" concept in accordance with art.141(1) of the EC Treaty.

Disability discrimination during the period of employment

39–131   [*Add to note 935: page* [1022]]
See now *Archibald v Fife Council* [2004] UKHL 32; [2004] I.R.L.R. 651 on the meaning of the concept of reasonable adjustment.

Trust and confidence and other implied duties

39–145   [*Add to note 993: page* [1029]]
Compare the application of the implied obligation in favour of a senior manager in *Horkulak v Cantor Fitzgerald International* [2003] EWHC 1918 (QB) [2004] I.C.R. 697.

[*Add to note 1001*]
Compare now *Crossley v Faithful & Gould Holdings Ltd* [2004] EWCA Civ 293; [2004] I.R.L.R. 377, in which it was held that there is no general obligation upon the employer to take reasonable care for the employee's economic well-being, and that the application of the criteria articulated in the *Scally* case did not require disclosure on the present facts. To similar effect has been *Lennon v Commissioner of Police of the Metropolis* [2004] EWCA Civ 130.

The extensions and limits of the implied obligation of trust and confidence

39–146   [*Add to notes 1008 and 1009: page* [1031]]
See now *Eastwood v Magnox Electric plc, McCabe v Cornwall County Council* [2004] UKHL 35; [2004] 3 W.L.R. 322, in which the House of Lords seeks authoritatively to draw the boundary between the area of exclusion of liability for breach of the implied term of trust and confidence envisaged in the *Johnson* case, and the area of pre-dismissal conduct on the part of the employer, apparently including conduct capable of being treated as constructive dismissal, within which liability for breach of the implied term may arise.

6. Termination of the Contract

(a) *Termination by Notice*

Form of Notice

[*Add to note 1043: page* [1034]] **39–152**
See, as to contingent or equivocal notice, *Rai v Somerfield Stores Ltd* [2004] I.C.R. 656, E.A.T.

(c) *Termination by Agreement or by Expiry of Fixed Period*

Termination by subsequent agreement

[*Add to note 1152: page* [1045]] **39–166**
Compare *Solectron Scotland Ltd v Roper* [2004] I.R.L.R. 4, E.A.T, as to the validity of a compromise agreement which could be regarded as limiting the application of the TUPE Regulations.

(e) *Assignment, Winding-up and Changes in the Employing Enterprise*

Transfer of employment: (2) the effect of the Transfer Regulations

[*Add to notes 1193 and 1198: page* [1049]] **39–171**
Compare *Martin v South Bank University*, Case C-4/01 [2004] I.R.L.R. 74, E.C.J., as to the application of the Acquired Rights Directive and the Transfer Regulations to early retirement benefits.

7. Remedies, and Rights, Incidental to the Termination of Employment

(d) *Damages for Wrongful Dismissal*

Damages for loss of earnings following wrongful dismissal

[*Add to note 1385: page* [1066]] **39–193**
See now *Harper v Virgin Net Ltd* [2004] EWCA Civ 271, in which it was held that damages for wrongful dismissal should not include compensation for the chance that, if the employee had not been dismissed with insufficient notice, she would have become time-qualified to make a claim for unfair dismissal.

Damages for injury to feelings or reputation

[*Add to note 1404: page* [1068]] **39–196**
An appeal to the House of Lords was allowed in *Eastwood v Magnox Electric plc* [2004] UKHL 35; [2004] 3 W.L.R. 322: see this Supplement, para.39–146, nn.1008 and 1009, above.

Deductions for Social Security contributions and benefits.

39–198   [*Note 1412: page* [1068] *Punctuation misplaced; the first three lines should read:-*]
Claims for damages for wrongful dismissal would seem not to be affected by
the recoupment provisions either of the Social Security (Recovery of Benefits)
Act 1997, which applies to "payments in consequence of any accident, injury or
disease" [etc.].

(e) *Equitable Remedies and Declarations*

Declaration and other remedies

39–203   [*Add to note 1441: page* [1072]]
Compare *Kaur v MG Rover Group Ltd* [2004] I.R.L.R. 279, Q.B.D., where a
declaration was granted of contractual entitlement not to be made redundant.

(f) *Employment Tribunal Jurisdiction*

Jurisdiction of employment tribunals in relation to contracts of employment

39–205   [*Add to note 1460: page* [1073]]
Compare *Peninsula Business Services Ltd v Sweeney* [2004] I.R.L.R. 49,
E.A.T., denying entitlement to commission payments which would normally
have accrued due at a date later than that of termination of employment, and
where the rules of the commission scheme excluded post-termination accrual.

8. UNFAIR AND DISCRIMINATORY DISMISSAL

(a) *Unfair Dismissal*

(i) *General Considerations*

Employments covered and employments specifically excluded

39–208   [*Add to note 1478 : page* [1075]]
As to the implicit exclusion of employees working abroad, see *Lawson v Serco
Ltd* [2004] EWCA Civ 12.

[*Add to note 1484: page* [1076]]
Compare *Wall v British Compressed Air Society* [2003] EWCA Civ 1762;
[2004] 2 All E.R. 200 in which it was held that an employee may have a "normal
retiring age" although in a unique position within the employing enterprise.

(ii) *Dismissal and Effective Date of Termination*

The effective date of termination

[Add to note 1538: page [1080]]

Compare *Fitzgerald v University of Kent at Canterbury* [2004] EWCA Civ 143; [2004] I.C.R. 737, in which it was held that a retrospective agreement did not validly alter the effective date of termination.

39–213

(iii) *Unfairness*

Introduction

[Add to note 1547: page [1081]]

As to the impact of the Human Rights Act 1998 on the adjudication of unfairness, see *X v Y (Employment: Sex Offender)* [2004] EWCA Civ 662; [2004] I.R.L.R. 625.

39–215

Reasonableness of dismissal

[Add to note 1578: page [1084]]

This should now be considered in conjunction with the provisions about statutory dispute resolution procedures, detailed in paras 39–258—39–262 of the Main Work. The provisions came into force on October 1, 2004.

39–217

Compensation for unfair dismissal: the compensatory award

[Add to note 1706: page [1094]]

The principle in the *Norton Tool* case was upheld on the appeal to the House of Lords in *Dunnachie v Kingston-upon-Hull City Council* [2004] UKHL 36.

39–233

9. REDUNDANCY PAYMENT AND PROCEDURE

(b) *Redundancy Procedure*

Consultation with the representatives of recognised trade unions or of employees

[Add to note 1879: page [1109]]

See, as to the making of the award, *Susie Radin Ltd v GMB* [2004] EWCA Civ 180; [2004] 2 All E.R. 279.

39–256

10. Statutory Dispute Resolution Procedures

The statutory dispute resolution procedures

39–259 *[Note 1902: page* [1111]]

The Employment Act 2002 (Dispute Resolution) Regulations 2004 were duly enacted on March 12, 2004 with the SI number SI 2004/752, to come into force on October 1, 2004.

[N.B. THERE ARE NO AMENDMENTS TO CHAPTER 40]

INSURANCE

2. Insurable Interst

Definition of insurable interest
   [*Update note 24: page* [1152]]   **41–004**
   O'Kane v Jones is now reported at [2004] 1 Lloyd's Rep. 389.

The relevance of the risk of financial loss

   [*Update note 31: page* [1153]]   **41–005**
   O'Kane v Jones is now reported at [2004] 1 Lloyd's Rep. 389.

Life Assurance Act 1774

   [*Update note 107: page* [1159]]   **41–012**
   O'Kane v Jones is now reported at [2004] 1 Lloyd's Rep. 389.

The Marine Insurance Act 1906

41–014   *[Update note 123: page* [1160]]
O'Kane v Jones is now reported at [2004] 1 Lloyd's Rep. 389.

3. THE EVENT INSURED AGAINST

(d) *The Nature of the Loss or Damage*

Nature of loss

41–025   *[Add at the end of note 188: page* [1167]]
Horbury Building Systems Ltd v Hampden Insurance NV [2004] EWCA Civ
418; [2004] All E.R. (D) 124, at [13]–[27].

[Add at end of note 194: page [1168]]
affd. [2004] EWCA Civ 277; [2004] Lloyd's Rep. I.R. 481.

4. *UBERRIMA FIDES*

The duty to disclose material facts

41–029   *[Update note 222: page* [1171]]
O'Kane v Jones is now reported at [2004] 1 Lloyd's Rep. 389.

[Update note 225: page [1171]]
O'Kane v Jones is now reported at [2004] 1 Lloyd's Rep. 389.

Scope of duty of disclosure

41–030   *[Add to note 238 at end of first sentence: page* [1173]]
WISE (Underwriting Agency) Ltd v Grupo Nacional Provincial SA [2004]
EWCA Civ 962; [2004] All E.R. (D) 356.

[Update note 240: page [1174]]
O'Kane v Jones is now reported at [2004] 1 Lloyd's Rep. 389.

Effect of non-disclosure or misrepresentation

41–035   *[Update note 272: page* [1177]]
Drake Insurance plc v Provident Insurance plc [2003] EWCA Civ 1834 is now
reported at [2004] 2 W.L.R. 530.

Affirmation

[*Add to the end of note 287: page* [1179]]
As to the affirmatory effect of a contractual notice of cancellation, see *Mint Security Ltd v Blair* [1982] 1 Lloyd's Rep. 188, 198; *WISE (Underwriting Agency) Ltd v Grupo Nacional Provincial SA* [2004] EWCA Civ 962; [2004] All E.R. (D) 356.

41–036

5. THE PARTIES

Broker

[*Add to note 325 after the reference to Jackson & Powell: page* [1183]]
As to the assumption of a duty of care, see *European International Reinsurance Co Ltd v Curzon Insurance Ltd* [2003] EWCA Civ 1074; [2003] 1 Lloyd's Rep. 793.

41–042

Lloyd's

[*Add to note 329 before the final sentence: page* [1184]]
Heath Lambert Ltd v Sociedad de Corretaje de Seguros [2003] EWHC 2269 (Comm); [2004] 1 Lloyd's Rep. 495.

41–043

6. THE CONTRACT OF INSURANCE

Payment of premium

[*Add to the end of note 378: page* [1190]]
As regards the position in respect of marine insurance, see *Heath Lambert Ltd v Sociedad de Corretaje de Seguros* [2003] EWHC 2269 (Comm); [2004] 1 Lloyd's Rep. 495; see above, para.41–043, n.329.

41–050

7. CONDITIONS AND WARRANTIES

Construction of terms

[*Add at the end of note 407: page* [1193]]
affd. [2004] EWCA Civ 622; [2004] Lloyd's Rep. I.R. 354, at [40]–[46].

41–053

Conditions precedent

[*Add to the end of note 412: page* [1193]]
As to a claims control clause in a reinsurance policy, see *Eagle Star Insurance Co Ltd v Cresswell* [2004] EWCA Civ 602; [2004] 2 All E.R. (Comm.) 244.

41–054

9. Claims

Details of loss

41–065   [*Add to the end of note 491: page* [1202]]
As to the adequacy of particulars provided by the assured, see *Super Chem Products Ltd v American Life and General Insurance Co Ltd* [2004] UKPC 2; [2004] Lloyd's Rep. I.R. 446, at [28]–[30].

The burden of proof

41–070   [*Line 5 of note 528: page* [1206]]
The *Kastor Navigation* case was affirmed, [2004] EWCA Civ 277; [2004] Lloyd's Rep I.R. 481.

Multiple Causes

41–073   [*Add to note 557 before reference to Kuwait Airways case: page* [1208]]
Midland Mainline Ltd v Eagle Star Insurance Co Ltd [2004] EWCA Civ 1042; [2004] All E.R. (D) 499.

Rateable proportion clauses

41–077   [*Update note 584: page* [1211]]
Drake Insurance plc v Provident Insurance plc [2003] EWCA Civ 1834 is now reported at [2004] 2 W.L.R. 530.

[*Update note 585: page* [1211]]
Phillips v Syndicate 992 Gunner is now reported at [2004] Lloyd's Rep. I.R. 426.

10. The Rights of the Insurer Upon Payment

Contribution

41–086   [*Update note 645: page* [1217]]
O'Kane v Jones is now reported at [2004] 1 Lloyd's Rep. 389.

[*Update note 647: page* [1217]]
O'Kane v Jones is now reported at [2004] 1 Lloyd's Rep. 389.

11. Specific Types of Insurance Contract

(a) *Liability insurance*

Employers' liability

[*Delete note 666 and substitute: page* [1219]]   **41–089**
Employers' Liability (Compulsory Insurance) Regulations 1998 (SI 1998/2573). As to reg.3, see *R (on the application of Geologistics Ltd) v Financial Services Compensation Scheme* [2003] EWCA Civ 1877; [2004] Lloyd's Rep. I.R. 336, at [20]–[22].

Statutory assignment

[*Delete the reference to Tarbuck case from note 669 and substitute: page* [1220]]   **41–090**
In the matter of OT Computers Ltd (in administration) [2004] EWCA Civ 653; [2004] 2 All E.R. (Comm.) 331.

[*Add to note 672 before 2nd sentence: page* [1220]]
See *Centre Reinsurance International Co v Curzon Insurance Ltd* [2004] EWHC 200 (Ch); [2004] 2 All E.R. (Comm.) 28.

(b) *Motor insurance*

Road Traffic Act 1988

[*Add to note 681 after first sentence: page* [1221]]   **41–091**
cf. Slater v Buckinghamshire County Council [2004] Lloyd's Rep. I.R. 432.

Third parties and uninsured drivers

[*Delete note 703 and substitute: page* [1223]]   **41–093**
The current agreement dated August 13, 1999 (and called "Compensation of Victims of Uninsured Drivers"), is between the M.I.B. and the Secretary of State for the Environment, Transport and the Regions, and applies to claims arising on or after October 1, 1999. It is effectively based upon the original 1945 agreement, with subsequent agreements in 1946, 1971, 1972 and 1988. A more complex scheme (first introduced in 1969) covers the position of untraced drivers. This is now governed by the Untraced Drivers Agreement dated February 14, 2003, the immediate predecessor to which was the 1996 Agreement. The M.I.B.'s liability under the 2003 Agreement is dependent on establishing that the untraced driver would have been liable to the victim and that that liability is of a kind required to be covered by compulsory insurance under the Road Traffic Act 1988. Applicants for compensation under these agreements, however, cannot rely on the doctrine of direct effect in the event that there is any shortfall in the cover provided by them and the cover required to be legislated by the United Kingdom by EC Directives 72/166, 84/5 and 90/232: *Evans v Motor Insurers' Bureau*

[1999] Lloyd's Rep. I.R. 30. However, in *Evans v Secretary of State for the Environment, Transport and the Regions* [2001] EWCA Civ 32; [2002] Lloyd's Rep. I.R. 1, at [4], the Court of Appeal indicated that the victim might have the right to enforce the Agreement pursuant to the Contracts (Rights of Third Parties) Act 1999. Clause 31(5) of the Untraced Drivers Agreement dated February 14, 2003, confirms that the Agreement is intended to benefit the victim. As to the level of compensation obtainable under the agreements, see *Evans v Secretary of State for the Environment, Transport and the Regions* (Case C-63/01) [2004] Lloyd's Rep. I.R. 391 (E.C.J.). As to the relationship between the M.I.B. and the Secretary of State, see *Sharp v Pereira* [1999] Lloyd's Rep. I.R. 242.

[*Add at end of note 705: page* [1224]]

In *Pickett v Motor Insurers Bureau* [2004] EWCA Civ 6; [2004] Lloyd's Rep. I.R. 513, the Court of Appeal considered whether the M.I.B. was liable under the 1988 Agreement where the claimant, who was also the owner of, but a passenger in, the vehicle, knew that the vehicle was uninsured. The court held that the claimant had not withdrawn her consent to be carried in the vehicle because she had not unambiguously required the vehicle to be stopped so that she could get out, thus permitting the M.I.B. to rely on an exception to liability.

(c) *Reinsurance*

Liability of the reinsurer

41–095   [*Line 4 of note 722: page* [1226]]

Assicurazioni Generali SpA v CGU International Insurance plc was affirmed, [2004] EWCA Civ 429; [2004] 2 Lloyd's Rep. I.R. 457.

CHAPTER 42

RESTRICTIVE AGREEMENTS AND COMPETITION

2. COMPETITION RULES UNDER THE EC TREATY

(b) *Article 81(1)*

Effect on trade between Member States

[*Page* [1242]]   **42–027**

The Commission has published *Guidelines on the effect on trade concept in Articles 81 and 82 of the Treaty*, OJ 2004 C101/81.

(c) *Article 81(3)*

Agreements likely to satisfy Article 81(3)

[*Page* [1243]]   **42–032**

The Commission has published *Guidelines on the application of Article 81(3) of the Treaty*, OJ 2004 C 101/97.

[149]

Block exemptions currently in force

42–034 *[Note 106: page* [1245]]
Regulation 240/96 was replaced, with effect from May 1, 2004, by Regulation 772/2004, OJ 2004 L 123/11.

(d) *Application of Article 81 to specific agreements*

Mergers

42–037 *[Page* [1247]]
Regulation 4064/89 was replaced, with effect from May 1, 2004, by Regulation 139/2004, OJ 2004 L 24/1.

Technology transfer agreements

42–056 *[Page* [1254]]
Regulation 240/96 was replaced, with effect from May 1, 2004, by Regulation 772/2004, OJ 2004 L 123/11.

(f) *Enforcement at the national level*

Effect of the Modernisation Regulation

42–067 *[Add at the end of the paragraph: page* [1259]]
The Commission has published a *Notice on the co-operation between the Commission and the courts of the EU Member States in the application of Articles 81 and 82 EC.*[191a]

[191a] OJ 2004 C 101/54

Causes of action in English law

42–071 *[Add to note 199, at the end: page* [1260]]
However, the Court of Appeal reversed the judgment of the High Court, and Crehan was awarded damages for the harm he had suffered: [2004] EWCA Civ 637; [2004] E.C.C. 28.

Role of national competition authorities

42–072 *[Page* [1260]]
The Commission has published a *Notice on Co-operation within the Network of Competition Authorities*, OJ 2004 C 101/43.

(g) *Enforcement at the Community level*

Commission investigations and adverse decisions

[*Line 12, after* "... *written and oral rights of defence": page* [1261]]   **42–074**
The Commission has adopted this implementing regulation, Regulation
773/2004, OJ 2004 L 123/18.

3. UNITED KINGDOM COMPETITION LAW

(a) *Introduction*

Reform of the law

[*Add, at the end of the paragraph: page* [1262]]   **42–077**
A number of statutory instruments have been adopted to amend the Competi-
tion Act in order to make it compatible with the principles of the EC modernisa-
tion package. See in particular the Competition Act 1998 and Other Enactments
(Amendment) Regulations 2004[213a]; The Competition Act 1998 (Land Agree-
ments Exclusion and Revocation) Order 2004[213b]; the Competition Act 1998
(Determination of Turnover for Penalties)(Amendment) Order 2004[213c]; and the
Competition Act 1998 (Appealable Decisions and Revocation of Notification of
Excluded Agreements) Regulations 2004.[213d]

[213a] SI 2004/1261.
[213b] SI 2004/1260.
[213c] SI 2004/1259.
[213d] SI 2004/1078.

(b) *The Chapter I Prohibitions: Agreements*

Effect on trade within the United Kingdom

[*Add, at the end of sub-paragraph (ii): page* [1266]]   **42–087**
The Commission has published *Guidelines on the effect on trade concept in
Articles 81 and 82 of the Treaty.*[225a]

[225a] OJ 2004 C 101/81.

[*Add at the end of sub-paragraph (iv)*]
The system of notifying agreements for individual exemption has been abol-
ished by the Competition Act 1998 and Other Enactments (Amendment) Regulations 2004.[227a]

[227a] SI 2004/1261.

Relevant differences between the Chapter I prohibition and EC law

42–091   [*Page* 1267]]
     The exclusion of vertical agreements from the Chap. I prohibition will be repealed with effect from May 1, 2005 as a result of the Competition Act 1998 (Land Agreements Exclusion and Revocation) Order 2004 (SI 2004/1260).

Schedule 2: competition scrutiny under other enactments

42–101   [*Add at the end of the paragraph: page* [1272]]
     Some amendments to Sch.2 are effected by para.49 of the Competition Act 1998 and Other Enactments (Amendment) Regulations 2004.[262a]

     [262a] SI 2004/1261.

Schedule 3: "general exclusions"

42–102   [*Add, at the end of the paragraph: page* [1272]]
     Some amendments to Sch.3 are effected by para.49 of the Competition Act 1998 and Other Enactments (Amendment) Regulations 2004.[262b]

     [262b] SI 2004/1261.

Repeal of the exclusion order for vertical agreements

42–115   [*Page* [1275]]
     The exclusion of vertical agreements from the Chap. I prohibition will be repealed with effect from May 1, 2005 as a result of the Competition Act 1998 (Land Agreements Exclusion and Revocation) Order 2004 (SI 2004/1260).

Sections 4 and 5: individual exemption

42–118   [*Page* [1277]]
     The system of notifying agreements for individual exemption has been abolished by the Competition Act 1998 and Other Enactments (Amendment) Regulations 2004 (SI 2004/1261).

Sections 12–16: notification

42–122   [*Page* [1278]]
     The system of notifying agreements for individual exemption has been abolished by the Competition Act 1998 and Other Enactments (Amendment) Regulations 2004 (SI 2004/1261).

(e) *Investigation and enforcement*

Penalties

[*Add to text after note 338: page* [1284]]   **42–139**
The maximum penalty is now calculated by reference to worldwide turnover
rather than UK turnover as a result of the Competition Act 1998 (Determination
of Turnover for Penalties) (Amendment) Order 2004.[338a]

[338a] SI 2004/1259.

(g) *The Competition Appeal Tribunal*

The Competition Appeal Tribunal

[*Add to line 9, after "... apply from June 20, 2003": page* [1286]]   **42–145**
The Competition Appeal Tribunal (Amendment and Communications Act
Appeal) Rules 2004[358a] amend the Competition Appeal Tribunal Rules 2003.

[358a] SI 2004/2068.

CHAPTER 43

SALE OF GOODS

[154]

3. TERMS OF THE CONTRACT

(a) *Conditions, Warranties, Misrepresentations and Puffs*

Misrepresentations external to the contract

[*Add to note 176: page* [1311]]   **43–046**
For a recent example see *Thompson v Christie Manson & Woods Ltd* [2004]
EWHC 1101 (QB) (attribution of vase by auctioneer without warning of non-
finality of attributions).

(b) *Implied terms*

(iii) *Implied Terms about Quality and Fitness for Purpose*

Satisfactory quality

[*Add to note 346: page* [1330]]   **43–086**
Bramhill v Edwards [2004] EWCA Civ 403 (American mobile home slightly
wider than UK regulations permitted; not of unsatisfactory quality, objective test
considered).

Reliance may be rebutted

[*Add to note 382: page* [1334]]   **43–096**
The *Britvic* case is discussed by Sealy [2003] C.L.J. 260.

Reasonably fit for purpose

43–097   [*Add to note 392: page* [1335]]
It has been held that the seller of a software package may be liable if he does not make clear, at least in general terms, that not all packages are compatible: *Brocket v DGS Retail Ltd* [2004] C.L. Jan. 322.

(v) *Exclusion of Terms Implied by Sections 13, 14 and 15*

Dealing as consumer

43–106   [*Add to note 431: page* [1339]]
The *R & B* case was followed in *Feldaroll Foundry plc v Hermes Leasing (London) Ltd* [2004] EWCA Civ 747 (Lamborghini for managing director of finance company: company dealt as consumer).

4. CONSUMER PROTECTION

(a) *Additional Remedies of Buyer in Consumer Cases*

Enforcement

43–124   [*Add to note 516: page* [1349]]
See Harris (2003) 119 L.Q.R. 541.

Rescission

43–127   [*Add to note 521: page* [1350]]
See a note on rescission under the Regulations by Hogg in [2003] S.L.T. 277.

(b) *Cancellation Rights*

Consumer Protection (Distance Selling) Regulations 2000

43–137   [*Page* [1354]]
The Consumer Credit (Disclosure of Information) Regulations 2004 (SI 2004/1481) (see para.38–070, above) do not apply to distance contracts (as defined in reg.1(2) of those Regulations).

(e) *Other enactments*

Advertisements etc

43–159   [*Amend the text to note 633: page* [1361]]
The Price Marking Order 1999 has been revoked and replaced by the Price Marking Order 2004 (SI 2004/102).

5. EFFECTS OF THE CONTRACT

(c) *Transfer of Title*

(i) *Sale by Person not the Owner*

Sales under special powers or court orders

[*Add to note 908: page* [1393]]   **43–233**
S.138B of the Supreme Court Act 1981 has been repealed by s.109(3) and
Sch.10 of the Courts Act 2003 and replaced by Sch.7, para.10 of that Act.

(ii) *Effect on Title of Writs of Execution*

Effect on title of writs of execution

[*Page* [1403]]   **43–260**
S.138 of the Supreme Court Act 1981 has been repealed by s.109(3) and
Sch.10 of the Courts Act 2003 and replaced by the provisions contained in Sch.7
to that Act.

6. PERFORMANCE OF THE CONTRACT

(b) *Rules Governing Delivery*

(ii) *Time for Delivery*

Waiver of delivery time

[*Add to note 1059: page* [1409]]   **43–275**
See also *Fleming & Wendeln GmbH & Co v Sanofi SA/AG* [2003] EWHC 561
(QB); [2003] 2 Lloyd's Rep. 473.

(c) *Examination and Acceptance*

Lapse of a reasonable time

[*Add to note 1182: page* [1424]]   **43–310**
The emphasis of *Jones v Gallagher* seems to be that the question is one of fact.
See also *Hawkins v C.D. Bramall plc*, HH Judge Dowse, [2004] C.L. June 94 (car
rejected after six days but buyer continued to drive it for nine months and 14,000
miles, during which car damaged in collision: held nothing to prevent reliance on
original rejection); *A.C. Daniels & Co Ltd v Jungwoo Logic*, Q.B.D. (HH Judge
Hicks Q.C., April 14, 2000 (injection mould: valid rejection after 13 months). On
Jones v Gallagher see Bradgate (2004) 120 L.Q.R. 558; and on *Clegg v Olle
Andersson* see Reynolds (2003) 119 L.Q.R. 544.

8. Remedies of the Buyer

(a) *Damages for non-delivery*

Damages where there is an available market

43–416   *[Add to notes 1821 and 1823: page* [1480]]
On the possible relevance of the buyer's lack of financial resources, see above
paras 26–095A—26–095D, 26–097.

(d) *Other remedies of the buyer*

Specific performance

43–466   *[Add to note 2124: page* [1513]]
See Harris, (2003) 119 L.Q.R. 541.

CHAPTER 44

SURETYSHIP

4. CONSTRUCTION OF THE CONTRACT

Impact of modern approach to construction.

[Add to text at end of paragraph: page [1555]] **44–057**

On the other hand, in *Vodafone Ltd v GNT Holdings (UK) Ltd*[277a] the High Court applied the "new approach" to construction found in *Investors Compensation Scheme Ltd v West Bromwich Building Society*[277b] to the construction of a guarantee. There a director of a company, company A, had signed on its notepaper a guarantee of the obligations of its subsidiary, company B. The guarantee was expressed to be for the benefit of company C. However, company B had entered an agreement not with C but with company D, which was in the same group of companies as company C. Company C was merely a holding company and no company in the group other than company D had entered such an agreement. In these circumstances, it was held that the guarantee was given by company A in respect of company C's liabilities to *company D*; the circumstances led the judge "to the conclusion that something went wrong with the drafting of the [guarantee] letter. . . . To construe it literally would be a commercial nonsense."[277c]

[277a] [2004] All E.R. (D) 194 (Mar.).
[277b] [1998] 1 W.L.R. 896.
[277c] [2004] All E.R. (D) 194 (Mar.) at [74] *per* Christopher Moger Q.C. sitting as a deputy judge of the High Court. *cf. Amalgamated Investment & Property Co Ltd (In Liquidation) v Texas Commerce International Bank Ltd* [1982] Q.B. 84 (guarantee expressed on its terms to cover loan by bank held in the "factual matrix" of the contract also to cover loan by bank's subsidiary).

6. DISCHARGE OF SURETY

(b) *Discharge of Surety through Discharge of Principal Debtor*

Discharge of debtor through debtor's breach of contract

44–085   [*Add text at end of paragraph: page* [1570]]
For example, in *Manx Electricity Authority v J P Morgan Chase Bank*[404a] the Court of Appeal held that where the main contract is breached by the principal debtor, a guarantor under a performance guarantee remained liable under it to the creditor even where the contract guaranteed had subsequently ceased to exist. "A repudiatory breach [by the debtor] will in the normal course of events lead to the termination of the repudiated contract (although of course it may not do so). It would be extraordinary if a performance guarantee was intended to case to operate in exactly the situation in which its beneficiary most needs it—when the contract has failed because the principal has repudiated it."[404b]

[404a] [2003] EWCA Civ 1324; 2003 WL 22187638.
[404b] *Ibid.*, at [37] *per* Rix L.J. See similarly at [47] *per* Chadwick L.J.

Discharge of debtor by operation of law

44–088   [*note 415: page* [1572]]
Hindcastle Ltd v Barbara Attenborough Associates Ltd [1997] A.C. 10 was applied in *Scottish Widows plc v Tripipatkal* [2003] EWHC 1874 (Ch); [2003] B.P.I.R. 1413.

(c) *Discharge of Surety through Variation of Contract between Debtor and Creditor*

Variation of contract between creditor and debtor

44–089   [*Add to text of note 418 after reference to Howard de Walden Estates Ltd v Pasta Place Ltd: page* [1572]]
Marubeni Hong Kong and South China Ltd v Government of Mongolia [2004] EWHC 471(Comm); [2004] All E.R. (D) 257 (Mar.) at [58]–[60].

(d) *Discharge of Surety on Other Grounds*

Altering the terms of guarantee

[*Add to second sentence after "held to be whether" in line 5: page* [1576]]   **44–099**
"there is an alteration which affects the very nature and character of the instrument" or

[*Note 457: page* [1576]]
Amend reference to *Raiffeisen Zentralbank Osterreich AG v Crosseas Shipping Ltd* to: [2000] 1 W.L.R. 1135, 1146–1148 *per* Potter L.J.

[*Add at end of text of note 457: page* [1576]]
    cf. Bank of Scotland v Henry Butcher & Co [2003] EWCA Civ 67; [2003] 2 All E.R. (Comm.) 557 at [72]–[74] where an alteration by some co-guarantors was held to be plainly beneficial to the others who were not as a result discharged.